NEATH
ENGINEMEN

Reminiscing Steam in South Wales

compiled by
Bryan King

THE OAKWOOD PRESS

© Oakwood Press & Bryan King 2009

British Library Cataloguing in Publication Data
A Record for this book is available from the British Library
ISBN 978 0 85361 691 7

Typeset by Oakwood Graphics.
Repro by PKmediaworks, Cranborne, Dorset.
Printed by Cambrian Printers, Aberystwyth, Ceredigion.

All rights reserved. No part of this book may be reproduced or transmitted in any form or by any means, electronic or mechanical, including photocopying, recording or by any information storage and retrieval system, without permission from the Publisher in writing.

Locomotive crew and shunters pose next to '517' class 0-4-2T No. 216 in Neath yard *circa* 1920.   *J. Williams*

Front cover: The interior of Court Sart shed in September 1963.
Roger Holmes/Hugh Davies Collection

Title page: A '57XX' class 0-6-0PT and its brake van awaits the 'right away' from Neath (Riverside) on 6th June, 1963.   *R.H. Marrows*

Published by The Oakwood Press (Usk), P.O. Box 13, Usk, Mon., NP15 1YS.
E-mail: sales@oakwoodpress.co.uk
Website: www.oakwoodpress.co.uk

Contents

Acknowledgements

R.A. Cooke (References from his *Track Layout Diagrams* and *GWR Atlas*)
Tudor Watkins (Historic information and photographs)
D.S.M. Barrie (Historical References)
Neath GWR Retired Railway Club Members
Neath Railway Historical Society Archive
Welsh Railway Research Circle members
Swansea Record Library (Maps)
Neath Museum
Michael Hale (Reference)
Alan Williams (Historical Information)
Robert Thomas (Photo collection)
Thomas Idris Lewis, Extracts from the *Ideal Miner*
Ian Allan Publications (Shed Allocations)
Rowland Pittard (Timetables)
E. Mountford (Swansea Docks)
E. Lyons (Swansea Docks)
Bob Grant (Photographs)

Rowland Pittard has helped me out with BR timetables, thanks to Tudor Watkins who has put many photographs into my domain, to Jack Jones who has given valuable insight into British Railways' goods workings. Although Jack is 88 years young his memory is extremely sound and he could remember train times with no hesitation. Not forgetting the typist Pat, my wife, who has spent many hours typing out the stories and facts for printing.

We, I say 'we' because the team of myself, John Last, Gerald Williams and Howard Jones have put people's memories down on record for historical reference. There obviously will be some minor infringements of fact but we hope that we have kept them to a minimum, but we are open to constructive correction and will listen to any suggestions to alter our factual content and amend our historical record accordingly. Have an enjoyable read.

Neath harbour in 1898. Just discernible is a Swansea-bound train crossing the main line timber bridge. *Neath Museum*

Introduction

The stories in this book have evolved from South Wales railwaymen who want to leave a record of memories that were carried out within their working days and nights and which have disappeared forever as we move into a different era.

I started work with British Railways at Swansea Eastern Depot in January 1953 as a cleaner. After taking up my position as junior cleaner and call boy at East Dock, most of my early work involved office duties, such as post boy, taking mail out to employees and walking to High Street station with the mail, also cleaning locomotives that were on shed for repairs and engines that were running out on afternoon shift duties. Locomotives that saw attention were '42XX', '72XX', pannier tanks of all descriptions, dock engines Nos. 1140, 1142, 1141 and 1152 come to mind, '66XX' tanks, Taff Vale No. 308 and No. 2166 ex-Burry Port & Gwendreath Railway.

After two weeks I lost my junior position when two other cleaners started and I progressed from cleaning wheels to tank and bunker sides. After six months I did little cleaning but was out firing on a regular basis; my first duty being with Percy Lloyd on 30 Target shunting duties outside the shed. The regular locomotive on this duty was No. 2166. When younger cleaners moved onto this duty I progressed onto other duties which were outside the shed and were kept for the junior cleaner. These were 26T South Dock pilot, above Victoria station and tripping to Swansea High Street. 27T saw Prince of Wales Dock duties, also 5T worked the Prince of Wales Dock keeping the tipplers full with coal for the coal hoists, 17T saw work on the Low Level over Wind Street, the fish market in the South Dock and transferring traffic from Victoria station Low Level, also working within the dock area.

'56XX' class 0-6-2T No. 6605 takes water at Neath in 1960. The engine was allocated to Aberdare shed and had worked in over the Vale of Neath line on a local passenger train.
R. Grant

One of the duties I enjoyed most of all was 31 Target at Port Tennant. We used to trip between South Dock High Level and Eastern Depot and tripping out to Jersey Marine hump yard with traffic from the Midland Yard. At this time I was the old-hand cleaner and was on 31T with driver Jack Bebell for some time. The engine on this duty was always a '94XX'; on the afternoon duty my girlfriend used to come for a ride, she was given an overall coat and a fireman's hat and looked like a young cleaner. Later my girlfriend who acted as junior fireman became my wife; Pat and I have now been married for 50 years.

Adjacent to the engine shed at East Dock was a vast area taken up with railway allotments which belonged to retired railwaymen and some serving staff when they could find the time. I can remember all the fencing surrounding the allotment was old boiler tubes, about five feet high and which ran for some distance. Also there were old redundant station and lineside corrugated huts that were used for shelters and old station seats that were of some comfort to men after toiling in their patch.

After two years a vacancy came up at Neath N&B and I applied for and got it and that was the end of my cleaning duties, or so I thought.

Here I went straight into the pilot link which had five turns, three at Neath Jn (Klondyke) and two turns at Neath N&B yard. I did not work these turns on a regular basis because I was moved into the freight link to cover holiday and sick leave, except for the night duty at the junction because the cleaners were not allowed to work the night turns.

After two years I was called up to the Armed Forces and spent time in Malaya and Germany, afterwards returning to my home depot of Swansea Eastern Depot. When Beeching came along I was put back to a cleaner's position in 1962 with about 20 others. I applied for a post in Margam as a carriage & wagon examiner and spent three weeks in Swindon works learning my new duties. I then moved to Margam Knuckle yard and stayed for about two years.

After that I transferred as a guard at Margam and worked duties covering the valleys around Margam and working as far as Severn Tunnel, Gloucester and Bristol on the main line. I then applied for a vacancy at Neath station as a guard and got it, and spent about a year at this position until the Neath depot was closed and moved to Margam. I was then made redundant because I did not want to return to Margam again.

This about covers British Rail service except for going into the steam preservation game and joining a group of boys to purchase a former Great Western Railway locomotive No. 9642 which came from Hayes scrap yard at Bridgend. I also got involved in footplate duties and became a fireman/driver at the Gwili, Swansea Vale and the Dean Forest railways.

I would like to take this opportunity to thank all who have participated in this book for historical reference, of course, not forgetting their wives who were part of that team; we could not have done it without them.

Bryan King

Chapter One

A Brief History of the Railways serving Neath

In 1826 a tram road, 8½ miles in length, was proposed from Seven Sisters to the Tennant canal at Aberdulais where an incline plane was planned. George Tennant was a major shareholder: it received Parliamentary consent but was not built due to financial restraints.

In 1862 the Dulais Valley Mineral Railway Company obtained an Act to build a mineral railway from Neath to Onllwyn, a distance of 10 miles. The Dulais Valley Railway then gained additional powers on 13th July, 1863, to change its name to the Neath & Brecon Railway (N&B) and also gain powers to extend to Brecon (Mount Street). A further Act, dated 29th July, 1864, authorized a branch into Banwen Colliery, also a branch from Colbren to Ynys-y-Geinon Junction in 1866 to meet the Swansea Vale Railway metals.

The line opened to Onllwyn Drum Colliery on 2nd October, 1864, then into Brecon on 3rd June, 1867 (thought to be the formal opening with regular trains from 8th June), although mineral traffic had been using the line to Brecon from September 1866. At Brecon a station was built at Mount Street where the N&B also gave permission for the Mid-Wales Railway passenger trains to use this station. The Merthyr trains used the small station at the Watton which was not suitable for the longer Mid-Wales trains.

On 1st March, 1871 a large station was built and opened at Free Street (Brecon) by the Brecon & Merthy Railway, the Mid-Wales trains soon transferring from Mount Street to this new station. The N&B trains started using this new station from 6th March, 1872, but still used Mount Street until 1874 when the latter closed to passenger traffic but was kept open as a good depot.

At Neath, the N&B at first (1864) built its own yard at Cadoxton, later called N&B yard. This connected to the Vale of Neath (VofN) line near the Low Level station, but the N&B could not use the mixed gauge track to work its coal traffic to Swansea docks because an early contract broke down. The Vale of Neath locomotives would pick up all the N&B traffic at Cadoxton. In 1867 passenger traffic worked from the station-cum-goods shed in Cadoxton yard until 1892 when a contract was struck with the Great Western Railway (GWR) to work the N&B's coal trains to Swansea docks and use the Low Level station for its passenger service.

The main contractor for the N&B was John Dickson who also had a timber yard and saw mill at Devynock, he also handled the rolling stock needs and most other matters; the Engineer was J. McKenzie. John Dickson took up residence in Cadoxton Lodge which was rented from George Tennant.

The Swansea & Neath Railway was opened in 1863 with James Rennie as the contractor. It ran from Neath Jn to Swansea Docks and was in operation before the N&B had opened. The N&B negotiated with the Swansea & Neath Railway to join their metals (which were mixed gauge) at Cadoxton Jn near the Low Level station. The Swansea & Neath became part of the VofN in 1863 and the GWR in 1865 after the latter absorbed the VofN company.

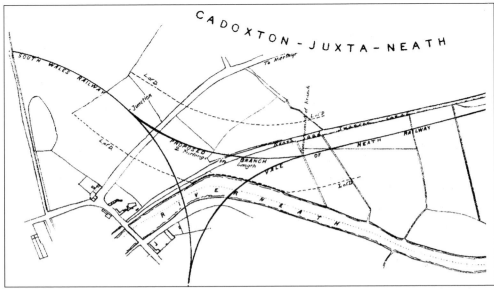

An 1847 plan to construct the west triangle to the South Wales Railway at Neath, from the Vale of Neath Act of 1846. *House of Lords Record Office*

The Neath triangle was opened in 1854 to give the Vale of Neath trains access to Swansea docks. Before this time trains had to reverse at Neath causing delays. The triangle ceased to be used for coal traffic after Briton Ferry docks opened in 1861. The triangle was removed in 1863 when the Swansea and Neath Extension Railway was built from Neath Junction to Swansea docks. The timber from the viaduct was used in the building of Neath station above the Low Level station in 1864, this station only lasting until 1877 when it was moved back to its original site. *Gerald Williams Collection*

The N&B line from Colbren to Ynys-y-Geinon was at last opened on 1st October, 1873 to goods and to passengers on 10th November, 1873, with an intermediate station at Ynisgedwyn (later 'Ystradgynlais'), the N&B having running powers over the Swansea Vale Railway to Swansea Docks. The N&B began running four trains a day from Swansea to Brecon, the Swansea Vale company running goods trains through to Brecon from 1st February, 1874. Later that year the Midland Railway obtained Parliamentary approval to lease the Swansea Vale Railway, which also gave them running powers over the N&B.

In 1877 agreement was reached with the Midland Railway that it would work all trains between Ynys-y-Geinon Jn and Brecon, the N&B then only working the Neath to Colbren section, although it did work coal traffic (destined for Neath) from Ynys-y-Geinon Yard to Colbren from 1903 onwards. The Midland ran three trains daily in each direction between Brecon and Swansea, some of which conveyed through coaches to/from Birmingham (until 1916). The Midland (now London Midland & Scottish Railway (LMS)) withdrew its trains on 31st December, 1930 when the GWR, which had taken over the N&B in 1922, extended its Neath-Colbren service to Brecon and ran two trains each way between Colbren and Ystradgynlais. The Ynys–y–Geinon Jn to Colbren branch closed to passengers on 12th September, 1932.

In about 1864 the GWR moved its Neath Town station to a new location above the Low Level station to which all the Vale of Neath passenger trains had been diverted in August 1863. The High Level station lasted until 4th June, 1877 when it returned to the old Neath station site which was renovated and extended and is in use today. The Low Level station had several names: in 1863 Neath station, 1864 Low Level station, 1924 Bridge Street and 1926 Riverside. By 1954 passenger trains used only one platform and in 1958 the canopies were taken down. Passenger trains to Pontypool Road were withdrawn on 15th June, 1964, on which date Riverside closed.

An engine shed was built at Neath N&B Yard in 1864, it was a small shed with a small workshop to the rear. The shed was extended by 1893, and again in 1913, in 1924 the GWR reorganized this shed and in 1947 it was rebuilt.

In 1875 a great flood took away the embankment at Seven Sisters. When it was built in 1864 the contractor John Dickson only built a culvert for the Nanthir stream under the line. After a few days of heavy rain the culvert blocked up with debris and the water rose up the embankment and eventually took a 210 ft section away down the valley leaving a momentous job for the rail gangs to repair. A viaduct now replaced the culvert and in 1878 another flood coming down the Nanthir stream caused little damage to any property.

In 1929 the GWR built three extra halts, Cadoxton Terrace, Penscynor and Pantyffordd, the first two near Neath, the latter just south of Onllwyn.

Neath & Brecon Stations Opened to Passengers
(All closed to passengers 15th October, 1962, except where otherwise shown)

Neath Low Level (VofN) 1st August, 1863 (for VofN trains, 1892 (for N&B trains). Closed 15th June, 1964
Neath (Cadoxton Rd) 3rd June, 1867 to 1892 (station in goods shed (*see map*))
Cadoxton Terrace Halt 18th March, 1929
Penscynor Halt 1st August, 1929

The western extension in 1860 showing the timber viaduct over the River Neath and the triangle spur to connect with the South Wales Railway. The Tennant Canal is in the foreground. *NRHS*

The timber-built Neath bridge. In the background a 'Buffalo' 0-6-0ST is crossing the viaduct on the Vale of Neath line with a passenger train *circa* 1874.   *Neath Antiquarians*

Old for new, Neath bridge when the timber bridge was rebuilt in 1905.   *Neath Antiquarians*

A pannier tank crosses the Vale of Neath's Neath viaduct with a passenger train. This structure replaced a timber viaduct in 1875.   *J. Davies*

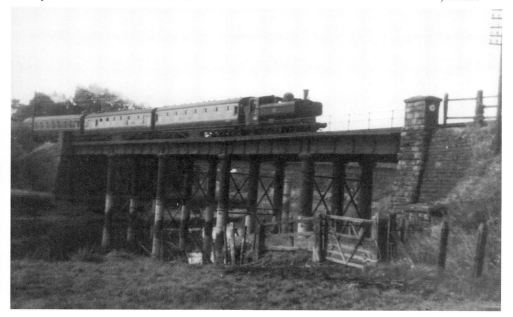

Resolven station, was just over five mile north-east of Neath on the Vale of Neath line. It was the largest station between Neath and Glyn Neath. This view dates from 1910.   *Author's Collection*

Clyne Halt on 8th September, 1926, shortly after it had opened. Rather more modest accommodation was provided for passengers here. Clyne Halt was between Neath and Resolven.   *GWR*

Cilfrew December 1888 (colliers) but public station 1st May, 1895
Cefn Coed Colliery Halt 8th September, 1930
Crynant 3rd June, 1867
Dillwyn 1928 (colliers)
Seven Sisters before 11th March, 1875
Pantyffordd Halt 2nd September, 1929
Onllwyn 3rd June, 1867
Colbren Jn 10th November, 1873 as 'Capel Colbren Jn', renamed 1874
Abercrave 2nd March, 1891. Closed 12th September, 1932
Ystradgynlais 10th November, 1873 as 'Ynisgedwyn', renamed 1st May, 1893. Closed 12th September, 1932
Craig-y-Nos 3rd June, 1867 as 'Penwyllt', renamed 1st February, 1907
Cray February 1870
Devynock & Sennybridge 3rd June, 1867
Abercamlais Private station 3rd June, 1867
Penpont Private station 3rd June, 1867
Aberbran 14th September, 1868
Cradoc 1st March, 1877
Brecon Mount St 3rd June, 1867 (closed completely 1877)
Brecon Free St 1871 (Brecon & Merthyr) N&B used from 6th March, 1872 instead of Mount St

Brief Particulars of the Railways around Neath & District

South Wales Railway (main line)
Opened 18th June, 1850 (broad gauge, engineer Brunel).
Traffic worked by GWR from inception, leased to the GWR in 1862, having been worked under an Agreement since 1851; amalgamated with the GWR in 1863.
Conversion to standard gauge in May 1872.

Vale of Neath Railway (broad gauge, engineer Brunel)
Opened from Neath to Aberdare 24th September, 1851, to Merthyr 2nd November, 1853, to Bwllfa Dare Colliery 1st June, 1857.
Connected with Pontypool Road on 18th April, 1864 (goods), 5th October, 1864 (pass) by opening by GWR of Middle Duffryn to Quakers Yard East. Amalgamated with the GWR 1st February, 1865. Converted to mixed gauge throughout by 31st December, 1864 (except Merthyr station,1867). Standard gauge by May 1872.
Branch closed for passengers 15th June, 1964 and steam finished by June 1965.
Aberdare shed closed 1964.
Neath Jn signal box closed 13th November, 1966.
Line closed Glyn Neath to Hirwaun Pond 2nd October, 1967. In 2009 the line to Glyn Neath has been 'moth balled' due to problems with geological faults at the new drift at Aberpergwm.

Neath & Brecon Railway (standard gauge, builder John Dickson)
Open to Onllwyn (goods only) 2nd October, 1864, regular goods from Sept. 1865.
Open to Brecon, (goods only) 13th Sept., 1866, open for passengers 3rd June, 1867 (Mount Street station), Mid-Wales trains used Free Street station from 1st May, 1871, N&B trains from 6th March,1872. Mount Street closed 1877.
Colbren to Ystradgynlais Branch opened 1st October, 1873 (goods), 10th November, 1873 (pass.), closed 20th February, 1967 except for stub from Abercrave Colliery to Colbren Jn closed 4th November, 1969.
Midland Railway took over the Swansea St Thomas to Brecon trains July 1877 to 31st December, 1930, the N&B then only working between Neath and Colbren Jn, but from 1903 also working coal traffic from Ynysgeinon Yard to Colbren Jn.

A busy station forecourt at Neath (General).   *Neath Antiquarians*

Neath (General) station in 1928 looking towards Swansea. The signal box was moved on 17th
July, 1929 to the Swansea end of the station.   *Neath Museum*

The Midland Railway was taken over by the LMS on 1st January, 1923.
GWR took over N&B 1st July, 1922, ran trains to Brecon from 1st January, 1931.
Craig-y-Nos to Brecon closed 15th October, 1962 and pass. services Neath-Brecon ceased same date. Brecon shed and station closed 31st December, 1962.
Colbren box closed 3rd April, 1967.
Craig-y-Nos (Hobbs) to Onllwyn went out of use 28th November, 1977 and closed in 1981. Neath to Onllwyn remains open for coal traffic including a new flow from Gwaun-Cae-Gerwen which comes to Onllwyn Washery for blending.

Swansea and Neath Extension Railway (builder James Rennie)
Open 15th July, 1863 (minerals), 1st August, 1863 (passengers) Neath Jn to Swansea Docks.
Acquired by the Vale of Neath in 1863, mixed gauge.
Amalgamated with the GWR on 1st February, 1865.
Passenger trains diverted from Swansea Wind Street station to High Street station from 1873, then from 1.10.1881 to 28.9.1936 to East Dock station, after which trains reverted to use of High Street station, reversing at Neath General.

South Wales Mineral Railway & Glyncorrwg Coal Co. (broad gauge, engineer Brunel)
Open from Briton Ferry to Tonmawr on 1st September 1861 (goods), to Glyncorrwg 10th March, 1863 (goods). Converted to standard gauge May 1872.
In addition to the mining operations the Glyncorrwg Coal Co. leased the S.Wales Mineral Rly (SWMR) under Act of 25th, May, 1855, the lease effective from 4th January, 1856. From 15th January, 1870 they worked the line but, following liquidation, the agreement was determined on 23rd October, 1878. The line was then worked by arrangement of the liquidator until the new Glyncorrwg Colliery Co. took over under agreements dated 19th March, 1880 and 27th November, 1880. This continued until 1st January, 1908 when the Port Talbot Railway & Docks Co. took over under the agreement of 14th December, 1907. Ynys-y-Maerdy Incline east of Briton Ferry was closed 1st June, 1910 and all traffic was diverted over Port Talbot Railway to Port Talbot Docks.
Passenger service from 1918-1930 (GWR bus service from 1930).
Colliers' (workmen's) train 1930-1958 Cymmer to Glyncorrwg North Pit; 1958 cut back to Glyncorrwg to Pit only. Workmen's service withdrawn October 1964. Line closed 24th August, 1970.

Briton Ferry (Court Sart) to Neath Canalside Station
Branch of the Rhondda & Swansea Bay Railway (engineers G. McKenzie & S.H. Yockney)
Open 14th March, 1895 with a push & pull service.
Branch closed to passengers 16th September, 1935, and goods 30th December, 1966 but part of the branch remained open for private siding traffic until 30th November, 1983.

Swansea District Line (Skewen East Jn to Morlais and Hendry Jns)
Built by the GWR and opened in sections in 1912 and 1913.
Neath Loop (Dynevor Jn North-Jersey Marine Jn North) opened 9th May, 1915, allowing through trains to be diverted onto the District Line at Court Sart Jn (Briton Ferry) and not needing to run through Neath.
BP Llandarcy Oil refinery opened 1917 with connections onto Jersey Marine Loop and thence the District Line at Lonlas Jn.
Morriston to Felin Fran branch opened 9th May, 1914, closed to passengers 11th June, 1956 and completely on 4th October, 1965.

Rhondda & Swansea Bay Railway (RSB) (engineers G. McKenzie & S.H. Yockney)
Opened (to Swansea) 14th December, 1894, to goods, to passengers 14th March, 1895.
Leased line to GWR in 1907, absorbed by GWR in 1922.
Swansea Riverside station closed from 11th September, 1933 (passengers used East Dock station until 28th September, 1936, thereafter High Street station being used).

A 1950s view of Skewen station looking towards Neath. *E. Gough*

Briton Ferry Road station on the Swansea and Neath Extension Railway in 1940. On the left is the Jersey Marine Hotel, it was built in 1864 for Captain Evan Evans by Neath builder John Taylor. *Author's Collection*

Court Sart station on the Rhondda & Swansea Bay Railway line. *Real Photographs*

Locomotive crew and shunter pose next to Swansea Harbour Trust No. 7 at Swansea (RSB) station. *South Wales Evening Post*

A general view of Briton Ferry showing the GWR in the foreground and the RSB in the distance.

Reflective Images, Port Talbot

This early aerial view of Briton Ferry dock shows how vast this area was. These docks provided considerable employment. Brunel's floating lock gate is prominent in this photograph.

Author's Collection

The docks, Briton ferry; the dock opened in 1861. This picture again shows Brunel's floating lock gate.   *Reflective Images, Port Talbot*

Duffryn Rhondda West to Cwmavon closed 2nd November, 1964
Duffryn Rhondda to Cymmer Afan taken out of use 24th August, 1970.

Port Talbot Railway & Docks
Act passed 31st July, 1894.
Contractors (Pearsons) started work in 1895.
Port Talbot dock opened 1837 (built by Emily C. Talbot), dock extended by railway company.
Line open to Maesteg 1st September, 1897 (goods), 14th February, 1898 (pass.) and line open to Pontyrhyll 14th February, 1898 (junction with GWR).
Port Talbot Railway & Docks and Ogmore Valley extension railway from Port Talbot dock to Cefn Jn opened 19th December, 1898. Running powers to Tondu over GWR line.
GWR worked line and trains from 1st January, 1908 and absorbed it in 1922.
Passenger trains cut back to Maesteg 12th September, 1932, withdrawn entirely on 11th September, 1933, closed to freight (Maesteg to Duffryn Yard) 31st August, 1964.
Locomotive shed at Duffryn Yard opened 1897, closed 2nd March, 1964.

Briton Ferry Docks
Briton Ferry Dock & Railway Co., Engineer I.K. Brunel, contractor Ritson. Dock opened 23rd August, 1861 used by the Vale of Neath Railway and South Wales Mineral Railway companies. (There had been an earlier 'Wharf' from 1852.)
GWR into dock 1865 (took over Vale of Neath Railway).
RSB Railway into dock December 1893.
Note: The dock company had severe monetary problems when building the dock and work had to stop in 1859. The Vale of Neath Railway invested £20,000 in the dock project and a further £40,000 in 1859 to enable the dock to be completed by 1861, thus allowing the Vale of Neath Railway coal traffic to be off-loaded at the dock.

Historical References
History of the GWR by E.T. MacDermot, Revised by C.R. Clinker.
Regional Railway History (South Wales) by D.S.M. Barrie
GWR Atlas 1947 and various Track Layout diagrams of the GWR and WR by R.A. Cooke (who also kindly checked the GWR element of the dates in these Brief Particulars).
The Neath & Brecon Railway by G. Briwnant Jones, D. Dunstone & T. Watkins
The Vale of Neath Line by G. Briwnant Jones & D. Dunstone
Tudor Watkins (Neath & Brecon)
Welsh Railway Research Circle
Neath Railway Historical Society

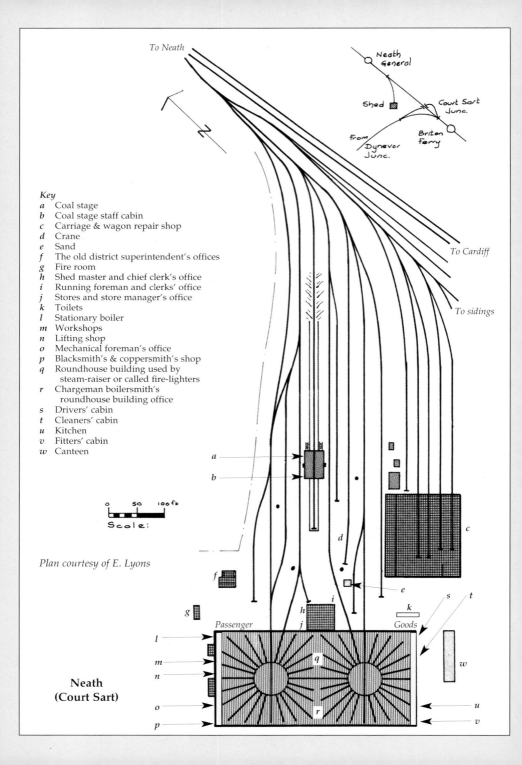

To Neath

Neath General

Shed

Court Sart Junc.

From Dynevor Junc.

Briton Ferry

To Cardiff

To sidings

Key

a   Coal stage
b   Coal stage staff cabin
c   Carriage & wagon repair shop
d   Crane
e   Sand
f   The old district superintendent's offices
g   Fire room
h   Shed master and chief clerk's office
i   Running foreman and clerks' office
j   Stores and store manager's office
k   Toilets
l   Stationary boiler
m   Workshops
n   Lifting shop
o   Mechanical foreman's office
p   Blacksmith's & coppersmith's shop
q   Roundhouse building used by
     steam-raiser or called fire-lighters
r   Chargeman boilersmith's
     roundhouse building office
s   Drivers' cabin
t   Cleaners' cabin
u   Kitchen
v   Fitters' cabin
w   Canteen

a

b

0   50   100 ft
Scale:

Plan courtesy of E. Lyons

c

d

f

e

g

i

h

j

Passenger

k

Goods

s

t

l

m

n

q

w

**Neath
(Court Sart)**

o

r

u

p

v

Chapter Two

Neath Engine Sheds
by Gerald Williams

Neath (Court Sart)

The first shed in Neath was the Vale of Neath shed near Neath station (*see overleaf*); built in 1862 it was 130 ft long by 30 ft wide and was a two-road shed with a second section of 250 ft by 50 ft with a through road which housed the repair depot. The construction was of stone with gable roof.

The main Neath shed was opened in the 1876 at Court Sart, about one mile south of Neath. It was located west of the main London to Swansea main line on land between the Swansea District line and the Neath canal. It replaced the two-road Vale of Neath Railway building nearby. Of brick construction, it was one of the earliest multiple turntable depots on the Great Western Railway, being preceded only by Wolverhampton (Stafford Road). It consisted of two 55 ft turntables all under one pitched roof, fed by a number of sidings adjacent to the coaling stage. The roundhouses had accommodation for some 40 locomotives, but there were usually about 60 locomotives on Neath's allocation. Part of roundhouse No. 2 was used as a workshop with facilities to repair about three locomotives. The coaling stage itself was enlarged in 1921 and was crowned by a large water tank that held some 90,000 gallons of water. The stage was serviced by a line that supplied coal wagons in typical Great Western style. Engines could be coaled on both sides of the stage. The decoking line lay to the south-west of the coaling stage, and there were sidings to accommodate locomotives in between duties. Adjacent to the shed was the carriage and wagon repair depot, and next to this a siding to store engines out of service, awaiting overhauls at Caerphilly or Swindon works. Usually the locomotives were given sacks to cover their chimneys to prevent rain erosion. Later the line was used to hold condemned engines waiting for disposal to scrap yards.

A signal box, Neath Engine Shed Junction, controlled movements between the main line and the shed. This box was opened in 1928 and closed after the end of steam in 1965. When Landore steam depot in Swansea was closed in June 1961, part of its main line allocation was transferred to Neath. To allow easier access to Court Sart shed a spur was built linking the Swansea District line with the shed. This allowed light engines from Swansea High Street station to travel via the Morriston branch to Felin Fran, thence over the district line to Court Sart.

Neath shed closed to steam in June 1965. Its remaining locomotives, one 0-6-2 tank and 10 0-6-0 pannier tanks were withdrawn and sent to Ward's scrap yard, Giants Grave, Briton Ferry, with the exception of Nos. 3654 and 4612 which were transferred to Cardiff East Dock depot. Luckily No. 4612 was sold to Woodham Brothers of Barry Docks for dismantling but was resold for preservation and is now to be seen operating trains on the Bodmin and Wenford Railway in Cornwall.

Locomotive allocation in 1947 was:

3455 *Starling* 'Bulldog' class 4-4-0

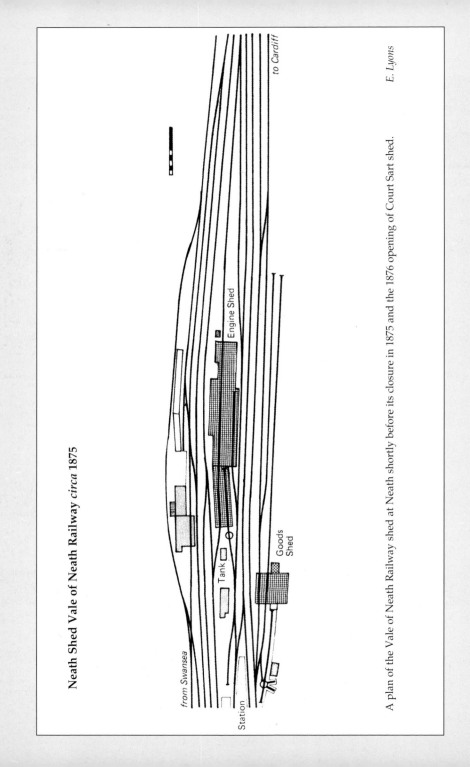

Neath Shed Vale of Neath Railway *circa* 1875

Station

Tank

Engine Shed

Goods Shed

from Swansea

to Cardiff

A plan of the Vale of Neath Railway shed at Neath shortly before its closure in 1875 and the 1876 opening of Court Sart shed.

E. Lyons

0-6-0 goods engine No. 381 stands at the coal stage at Court Sart in 1918. *Gerald Williams Collection*

From left to right: guard Bill Beer, fireman Tom Rees and driver Tom Anthony pose with South Wales Mineral Railway 0-6-0ST No. 3 at Court Sart shed in 1918. *Gerald Williams Collection*

A view inside the roundhouse at Court Sart in 1958.   *Gerald Williams*

Ex-Lancashire & Yorkshire Railway 'Pug' 0-4-0T No. 51218 in the roundhouse at Court Sart. The 'Pug' spent most of its working life in the Manchester area. In 1962 it was transferred from Bristol to Swansea East Dock. It was sent to Neath for storage in 1964 and was subsequently preserved and survives on the Keighley & Worth Valley Railway.   *Norman Jones*

Side tanks
75, 4232, 4252, 4259, 4274,4284, 4288, 5225, 5239, 5242, 5254, 8104, 6613

Pannier tanks
2192, 906, 1855, 2722, 2797, 1715, 3611, 5703, 5720, 7742, 7757, 7767, 7786, 8715, 8775, 9734, 9750, 9783

One of our Historical Society members is a retired British Rail (BR) steam fitter who worked at Neath shed. Gerald Williams, who comes from a long-standing railway family, joined BR as a steam fitter in 1960 and went to Neath Court Sart shed to become a running shed fitter. Gerald's work was mostly on engines not in steam which had been put off for repair which consisted of packing glands and pistons, attention to worn side rods and connecting rods, adjusting brake rodding and changing brake blocks. He also removed bearing caps to examine the bearing surfaces on the big ends and examination of the eccentric linkages for wear. Bigger jobs entailed lifting out wheel/axles in the lifting shop and examining bearing surfaces for wear, also changing springs and repairing ashpan wear.

Minor boiler work was also carried out, retubing, stays, and superheater work was ongoing at the depot, parts were cleaned with a steam lance. As might be expected there was a lot of grease around; boiler washouts were also part of his job.

The coppersmith did all the welding and pipe work, there was a considerable amount of pipework on a locomotive and running repairs were necessary. Also fitters used to have to go inside the water tanks unblocking and cleaning to make running repairs to the component parts of the water systems. Touch-up painting was done by the carriage and wagon boys who came over from the wagon works next door.

Internal workshop facilities at Court Sart were: lifting shop, gantry for lifting, stationary steam boiler for working machinery on a belt system, which also fed the carriage and wagon repair shop driving its machinery.

BR Standard Pacific No. 70018 *Flying Dutchman* receives attention at Court Sart from fitter Roy Anthony and fitter's mate Dick Richards in 1954.   *Gerald Williams*

HRH Princess Margaret visited Port Talbot on Thursday 26th April, 1956 to open the new sea wall. Fitters Roy Anthony and David Shorney pose with standby engine 2-6-2T No. 4169 at Neath (Court Sart) shed.
Gerald Williams

Matthew Arnold Davies at Neath shed wagon repair yard in 1946 (*left*) and 1952 (*right*).
(Both) Gerald Williams

Graham Jeffery with his bicycle by the sand house at Court Sart in 1949. Prairie tank No. 4169 is on the goods road.
Gerald Williams

Railway staff next to a Toad brake van at Neath.

Gerald Williams

Staff pose next to 0-6-0PT No. 7767, with shed driver David Williams standing *left*, in Neath carriage shop yard in 1958.

Gerald Williams

Neath shed fitting staff in 1962. *Gerald Williams*

Court Sart's ashes crane. *Gerald Williams*

A view from alongside the coaling stage road at Court Sart looking towards the double roundhouse *circa* 1963.   *H.B. Priestley/R. Read Collection*

Pannier No. 3654, based at Neyland, refuels at Court Sart's coaling stage on 24th April, 1965.
A. Evans

0-6-0PT No. 4653 outside the main office block at Court Sart.   *Gerald Williams*

The final day of steam working over the Vale of Neath line, 13th June, 1964 (*see page 121*). Shed staff stand next to the smartened-up 0-6-0PT No. 4639 prior to it working the final train of the day, the 9.10 pm to Pontypool Road. From left to right are: ?, Elvid Davies (*on engine*), shed foreman Mr Duggan, loco crew from Aberdare (*between buffers*), ? *(on engine)*, Gronwy Jones, Don Buttle, Ossie Parry and Sid Homes. The 45 ton breakdown crane is on the left.

Norman Jones

'42XX' class 2-8-0T No. 5221 stands in a line of locomotives which have been taken out of service. Five of the '1101' class 0-4-0Ts can also be seen.   *Gerald Williams Collection*

'1101' class 0-4-0T No. 1105 out of service at Neath. It was built for the GWR by the Avonside Engine Co. in 1926. The class was built to replace ageing Swansea Harbour Trust tanks and they spent most of their working lives operating from Danygraig shed. All the class were sent to Ward's at Briton Ferry for scrapping with the exception of No. 1101 which went to Cohen's at Morriston.   *Gerald Williams Collection*

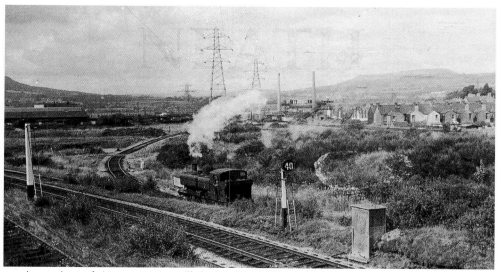

A pannier tank is seen coming off shed at Neath (Court Sart) in 1962 on the new exit road installed the previous year to help with the influx of locomotives from Landore.   *C. Read*

Duffryn Yard-allocated '56XX' class 0-6-2T No. 6616 passes Court Sart shed (in the distance) as it proceeds along the RSB line towards Court Sart station and Briton Ferry in 1962. The shed spur is to the right.   *C. Read*

Neath (Bridge Street) ex-N&B *circa* 1950s

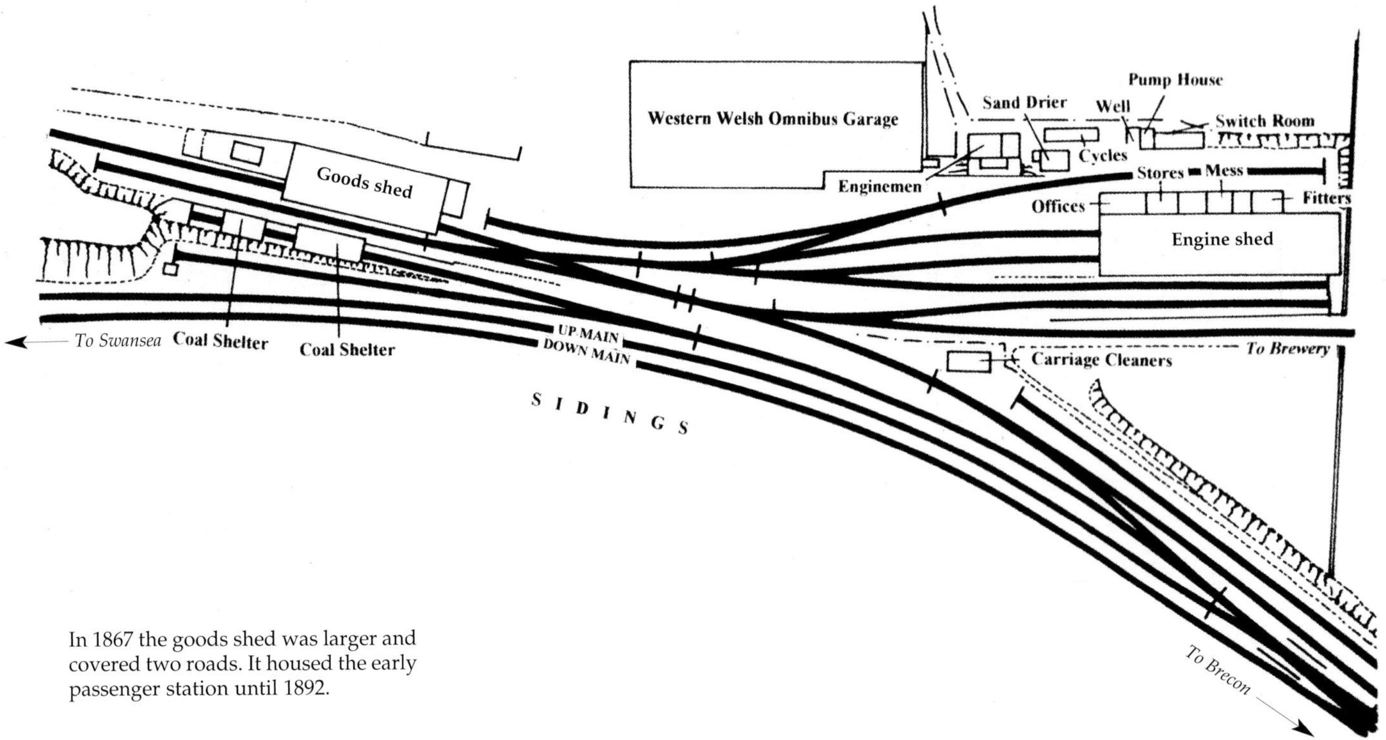

Western Welsh Omnibus Garage

Pump House

Switch Room

Fitters

Mess

Stores

Engine shed

Sand Drier

Well

Cycles

Offices

Enginemen

To Brewery

Carriage Cleaners

To Brecon

Goods shed

Coal Shelter

Coal Shelter

UP MAIN

DOWN MAIN

S I D I N G S

To Swansea

In 1867 the goods shed was larger and covered two roads. It housed the early passenger station until 1892.

GWR '1701' class 0-6-0PT No. 1715 outside Neath (N&B) shed on 28th May, 1939. This engine was built as a saddle tank at Swindon works in 1891 and was sold to the N&BR in 1914, becoming N&BR No. 16. On Grouping the engine returned to GWR stock where it carried its original running number until withdrawal in October 1949. *R.W. Rush Collection*

Neath (N&B)

The Neath & Brecon Railway shed opened in 1864 at Cadoxton Junction to accommodate the small N&B fleet. It was of timber construction and consisted of four roads with a two-road carriage shed built alongside. The shed was demolished on 8th March, 1946 when work started on a new shed.

The new structure was very different from the usual Great Western pattern as a GWR officer had adopted the idea from French practice. The shed incorporated a radical new method of construction using stressed and moulded concrete with brick and fill sections. A section of the N&B yards (New Sidings) was taken over as a casting site to formulate the smoke shutes for the roof of the new shed.

There was a reduction of shed roads from four to two, the shed yard was altered and one point was taken out. A block was built to accommodate the office, stores, mess room and fitters. Work on the new shed was completed by 9th October, 1946. Staff levels at the time were: one shed foreman, one clerk, 25 engine crew, four cleaners, 15 shed staff, and four fitters. The weekly coal consumption at the shed was 85 tons.

The shed's paint shop became the GWR bus depot. In April 1930 the bus depot passed to Western Welsh. This view shows the staff at the time of the hand-over in 1930. *K. Reason*

View of the new N&B shed under construction on 15th April, 1946. The smoke vents (*below*) were loaded onto wagons and worked into the new shed and then craned onto the roof.

(Both) GWR

A general view of the new shed in May 1952 showing a number of pannier tanks. *Author's Collection*

Neath's N&B shed with '42XX' class 2-8-0T No. 5222 being prepared for duty in 1963. *R. Grant*

Glyn Castle colliery, Resolven.   *Author's Collection*

The colliery shunting engine at Glyn Castle with colliery staff.   *Author's Collection*

Train Working Neath N&B Shed 1956/7 Timetable

am

4.15	Goods. Return with 6.35 Colbren workmen, arrive Neath 7.20.
6.00	Workmen Colbren. Arrive 6.49. Return 8.10 passenger, arrive Neath 8.48.
6.25	Goods, arrive Onllwyn 7.45. return 9.20 Onllwyn Goods, arrive Neath 10.23.
8.25	Passenger to Brecon arr. 10.09 am return with 11.00 Brecon to Neath Passenger. Arrive 12.39.
9.10	Goods to Colbren. Trips to Ynysygeinon Yard for Colbren traffic, transfer Brecon traffic to Brecon goods train (2.15 pm). Return with 3.20 goods from Onllwyn to Neath N&B Yard, arrive 4.31 pm.
9.10	Banker, return as ordered by Control.
9.30	Neath Jn to Resolven Tripper ('Jazz').*
10.10	Goods to Onllwyn, arrive 11.28. Returns with 1.10 pm goods arrive N&B Yard 2.38 pm.
10.10	Banker to above returns with 12.15 pm goods from Onllwyn, arrive Neath N&B Yard 1.40 pm.
10.35	Brecon to Colbren goods, arrive 1.30 pm. Return 2.15 pm, arrive Brecon 4.11 pm.
11.35	Goods to Colbren, arrive 1.45 pm. Return 3.00 pm passenger (workmen) arrive Neath 3.43 pm.

pm

12.40	Goods to Colbren. Return via Ynysygeinon, St Thomas, Swansea Docks, arriving Neath 7.05 pm.
1.45	Goods to Onllwyn, arrive 2.50 pm. Return with 4.05 pm Onllwyn goods, arrive Neath 5.35 pm.
2.15	Goods worked to Swansea Docks or as ordered by N&B Control.
2.30	Neath Jn to Resolven Tripper ('Jazz') 2nd trip; return by 6.20 pm.*
4.10	Passenger to Brecon arrive 5.51 pm. Return 6.20 Brecon to Neath, arrive Neath 7.54 pm.
5.15	Goods to Onllwyn, arrive 6.18 pm. Return with 7.30 Onllwyn goods, arrive Neath 8.31 pm.
9.40	Passenger to Colbren, arrive 10.26 pm. Return with 12.05 am goods from Onllwyn, arrive Neath 1.20 am.

Notes:

* Neath Jn to Resolven Tripper ('Jazz').

N&B set book on 8.15 am, Prep Loco (Pannier). Leave shed 9.15 am, run light engine to Neath Jn up side, pick up train with N&B guard.

Leave Neath Jn 9.30 am. Arrive Resolven 9.50 am, then shunt George Kent (now Cam Gears) then work to Aluminium Works, put off Aluminium domestic traffic, take out traffic and work over to Glyn Castle Colliery and shunt yard.

Leave Resolven Glyn Castle with train at 1.10 pm, arrive Neath Jn down side at 1.30 pm. Engine and van to up side, pick up 2nd trip (usually pools) and depart at 2.30 pm for Resolven, arriving at 3.40 pm (time allowed to shunt at Ynys Arwed colliery, Melyn Court).

In afternoon, shunt station goods yard and then make up load from Glyn Castle Colliery for return trip, leaving Resolven Glyn Castle at 5.15 pm. Arrive Neath Jn down side at 6.20 pm, loco to shed.

Appendix Three gives details of the duties carried out by the various members of shed staff.

Two views of '56XX' class 0-6-2T No. 5695 of Treherbert shed. The locomotive had become derailed outside Neath station and the breakdown crew were called to redress the situation.

(Both) Norman Jones

Neath Breakdown Gang

Neath steam shed breakdown gang area of cover was from Port Talbot to all of West Wales. The Neath crane of 45 tons would cover all big lifts in the area like track relaying, bridge repair and breakdowns. A typical breakdown gang would be a total of eight men, one of the gang would be a first aider, one man was in charge of tools and food. The gang members might have to carry packing and the jack for lifting an engine or wagons back on the rail some distance. If the crane was required the crane would have its own gang, a driver and two assistants who helped with any lifting and placing the packing to take the crane stabling bars for balance on a lift.

Typical breakdown train formation was, locomotive, crane, tool coach, sleeping, dining coach and guard's van. Crane drivers at Neath 1956-1964: Jack Morgan, Jack Cardiff, Walter Adams, Will Sanders. Breakdown gang members: R. Adams, B. Rendall, P. Jenkins, N. Jones, D. Williams, W. Hughes, H. Bazley, G. Thomas, A. Jenkins, T. Hughes, W. Smith, A. Brain, R. Lloyd, B. Conners, G. Williams, D. Preston, G. Jones

The man in charge of the breakdown was called breakdown inspector. These were: Jack Dyer 1955-59, Bill Jones 1959-1965 with Nat Lodwick 1956-61, Albert Williams 1961-63, Bernard Conners 1962-63, Arthur Gollop 1963-66 as foremen.

One breakdown involving an engine and 10 coal wagons at Felin Fran needed the 45 ton crane, and gangwork carried out by lifting wagons by jack and packing blocks of hard wood, taking two men to lift and carry, from the tool coach. Most of the work was done by jacking and re-railing. This job turned out to be a hard one which took three days to complete, and a lot of handling of equipment to and from the tool coach. This is the method used for most types of breakdowns and was carried out like this for many years and is still used today in some cases if the crane cannot get near the site of the breakdown.

Neath (Court Sart) Shed Duties

Link 1	Passenger Link
	Pontypool
	Aberdare
	Treherbert
	Trecynon Milk Trains
Link 2	Goods Link (1)
Link 3	Goods Link (2)
Link 4	Pilot Link
	Pilots Briton Ferry (2)
	1 Court Sart Yard
	1 Steel Works/Docks
	Pilots Felin Fran
	1 Down Side (trips to High Street)
	1 Up Side (trips to Mond)
	Pilots Neath Yard (3)
	1 West End
	1 East Beat
	1 Works Pilot
Link 5	Shed Link
	Shed Pilot
	Prep Duties

Loco Coal

The normal coal requirements of South Wales steam sheds was the good old Welsh steam coal and if everything was in order the engine concerned should not have any problems steaming, the excellent steaming qualities of the coal made the fireman's work reasonably straightforward.

There was a time when steam coal was limited and processed coal was brought in with disastrous results; we had ovoids and block processed coal and goods engines were struggling for steam everywhere.

The best coal was kept for main line passenger work and the processed coal was kept for the goods engines. It did not last long and to get rid of it it was mixed with Welsh coal for some time until the reserves were depleted.

The other type of coal we tried was what we called 'snap and rattle', it was English coal and burned very fiercely and was extremely hot and the ashes went to a very fine dust and made it easier for the firedropper, but it burned very quickly and you were shovelling twice as much, obviously using twice as much coal as normal Welsh coal. Again this coal was mixed with Welsh coal to solve the problem.

But the good old Welsh steam coal always got the best results.

Driver Tom Anthony and fireman Alan Davies pose next to '42XX' class 2-8-0T No. 4246 in Neath yard. Notice the loco coal wagon immediately behind the locomotive.

Gerald Williams

Chapter Three

Firing Techniques

Pilot Turns

When allocated to pilot duties the engine, usually a pannier tank, did not require elaborate firing techniques. After leaving the shed you would build up your fire at the back end and keep the front end low, also keeping the boiler water level in the gauge glass between ½ and ¾, this would leave room to keep the engine quiet. A full boiler would inevitably lead to the engine priming, that is blowing water through the cylinders and out of the chimney. The driver would not be happy with this situation, as he would have to open the cylinder cocks and then his viewing capacity would be reduced to almost nil.

Shunting on some turns would possibly be seven hours out of an eight hour shift and within the confines of the same yard it could be a little boring. At food breaks, usually about 40 minutes, the fire would be worked very low at the front end to allow cold air to work through the bars with the dampers closed and the boiler full. You could open the cocks, put the handbrake on and leave the engine quite safely knowing that it would be okay and would not 'blow off'.

After you had returned from the shunters cabin to resume shunting the fire would have gone out at the front and because you had kept the back end high with coal you could now push this over the front end, and rebuild the back end with fresh coal. If the steam pressure had dropped, you could excite the fire a little with the blower to raise the steam pressure to start shunting duties. If you were taking the engine to shed you would then work the fire as low as possible without drawing air through the bars to keep the fire-dropper happy.

Branch Line Working

What I found worked well on pannier tanks on the N&B was the saucer type fires which the N&B drivers said was the best to use. The work involved on the branch was entirely different to the pilot turn firing techniques. With the saucer pattern firing you would end up at Brecon with a reasonably high fire around the sides, back and front ends, with a low middle section. If you had a layover and you had to keep the engine quiet, you would work your boiler down to half a glass. By the time you had run round the train the fire had cooled down a little, you would drop the dampers, get the pricker out and clear the fire from the middle of the box to allow cold air to be admitted. This kept the engine reasonably cool and quiet (not 'blowing off') and if the pressure did rise you had room in the boiler to keep the engine quiet, that is by putting on the injector you would knock the steam pressure back.

Ten minutes before you were due away you would put the bar through the fire to clear the bars and start building up the fire again, and if required put on a little bit of blower to excite the fire.

0-6-0 pannier tank No. 7767 on Briton Ferry-Court Sart pilot duties. *Norman Jones*

A Llanelly crew in relaxed mood on the footplate of mogul No. 5335. They are waiting for the 'right away' from Neath station. *Norman Jones*

But different firemen had their own ideas on firing techniques and if something worked well for them, you accepted that, but the only problem with working a big fire was that if you had a box full of fire and had a lay-over you had a problem keeping the engine quiet.

Main Line Goods

Main line goods work, usually with a '42XX' class engine where you worked the locomotive to a point then had relief, needed a very high back-end fire and a low front end. The reason for this was that when climbing banks like Stormy and Llanharan, for example, you needed a heavy fire to take the blast and a low front end to keep the heat required to steam well, but not too low so you would draw air. It was important to have good steaming coal; on some occasions we had bad coal and had to work hard to maintain steam pressure and this is where your firing skill came in. It was reasonably straightforward on good coal, but if you had bad coal it was very hard work and would tax your ability to keep going. On one or two occasions the driver would say, 'Come over here mate, I'll give you a break'; that was if you had a good driver. You were a team and if you were to succeed team work was imperative.

'42XX' class 2-8-0T No. 4275 at Neath (Low Level) with a train of pools in June 1962.
Tudor Watkins

A view of the backhead showing the footplate controls on a preserved '28XX' class locomotive.
Author

Main Line Fast Running Freight

My experience on main line locomotives is limited and the only time we used to get them was on back working control turns from Severn Tunnel Jn. Engines that I can remember working were 'Halls', '28XX', Moguls '63XX', 'ROD', '9Fs', usually to Cardiff Newtown, and the engine would then run light to Tyndall Street engine reception roads where it was left, a set of men coming up from East Dock shed to take the engines to shed.

One trip I can remember quite clearly was with an old ROD (Robinson design) engine. The train inspector in the relief cabin at Severn Tunnel shouted out, 'East Dock control set make their way to the hump reception roads, your train has arrived'. When we got outside a suited gent came up to us and showed the driver a footplate pass so he could ride with us to Cardiff. We walked over to the reception roads meeting the Swindon men midway. They said, 'Rough old engine, boys'. My driver said, 'Looks like you have to earn your keep, mate'. When we got in view of our train the engine was a decrepit old ROD blowing steam from everywhere.

We climbed up onto the footplate and the first thing we noticed was the tender was half full of ovoids, and the cab area was covered in dust. The fireman had washed down the footplate but it was evident that we were going to have a dusty ride. The fire was satisfactory and was up behind the doors and reasonably flat all the way to the front of the box, steam pressure was good and the water in the glass was healthy.

We eventually got the road and we moved off with a mixed load with what looked like a lot of conflats (wagon holding containers) to the rear of the train.

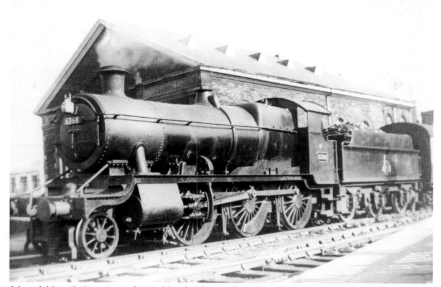

Mogul No. 6368 waits to leave Neath (General) with a passenger train over the Vale of Neath line to Pontypool Road.   *Norman Jones*

The guard gave us the tip and we were off from the reception road down the loop to Tunnel West box with the large West yards to the left of us. We were held up at the bottom of the loop, a passenger went by, the loop to main board dropped 'off' and we were out on the main line. This was unusual because we would normally go down the avoiding lines through to Newport East yards.

My mate opened up, I closed the fire doors, I looked out and there was steam leaking everywhere. At this point I was working the fire down and would probably not add too much coal because we were only going to Cardiff, and then to shed. I got the pricker out and examined the fire and it seemed to indicate that we had some clinker to deal with. I got the bar out and pushed it through and after some work it seemed all right, the steam seemed to be holding, but as soon as you put the injector on, the steam pressure would drop back. I put the blower on and this did help and it seemed to hold its own. I examined the fire and realised that I would have to put coal on to get to Cardiff. By this time my mate was beginning to run the train and we picked up speed. This brought problems that we had not expected, the wind was whipping up coal dust from the tender into the cabin and the old engine was clonking dreadfully, as the ROD would. Our passenger said that the conditions were extremely bad and asked how often we had these problems, the driver said not too often.

Tyseley-allocated 'ROD' class 2-8-0 No. 3023 runs into Neath yard from the Vale of Neath line.
Norman Jones

We were now running into East Usk and the suited gent asked if he could get off at Newport because he could not stand these conditions any longer. We ran into Newport over the river bridge and into the central roads where we were stopped by a signal. The suited gent got off covered in coal dust. I asked the driver who he was but he replied that he didn't know. We both laughed, realising that he had witnessed the downside of loco work.

We eventually got the road and ran up the slight incline into Gaer Tunnel and down the relief line to Pengam. Here I examined the fire and put the pricker in to level it off, the injector was on and steam pressure was not very good, but it was the end of our run, and the fire was just right. We put our train off at Newtown West and ran light to Long Dyke and into Tyndall Street loco siding and left the engine against four others waiting to be ferried to East Dock. We walked back to Cardiff General to travel home 'on the cushions'.

Another trip was working back from the Tunnel on a control turn and relieving Swindon men on the hump yard reception road. Finding a '9F' there, we climbed up on to the footplate and it was my first time on this type of locomotive. We found it very user-friendly with nice seats, a covered-in cab, screw dampers; when I looked into the firebox the fire was up to the firehole door. I said to my mate, 'He's left us a big fire', but he said, 'No, the firebars are just under the doors, it's got a very shallow box back end, keep the back end up'. We had a long string of banana vans for Barry Docks and we were getting relief at Canton on Penarth Curve. We had a fast fitted headcode up and we were expecting to run this train. I put about six shovels behind the doors and examined the front end, it looked all right. I put the pricker in to get the feel of the grate and realised that the fire was quite thick. The signal dropped 'off', down the loop to Tunnel West and immediately the main line board came 'off' and we were away. Within no time we were passing Llanwern, with the engine 'blowing off'. I put the injector on, opened the doors and we ran into East Usk then through the centre roads at Newport station. This was a first class locomotive. The driver opened up going through Newport station making an impressive bark from the chimney, we ran with distants 'off' through Marshfield into Pengam main, and down into Newtown East where we had a distant signal check. I looked at my fire which was still reasonably sound but decided because I was having relief I put 12 shovels around the box and built the back end up. There was black smoke belching from the chimney as we approached Newtown West, as we slowed down still on the main line the board drops 'off' and my mate opens up. The brakes are still dragging after the brake application but we finally pick the train up and run into the incline into Cardiff station. I put six more shovels around the back end and closed the door.

We pounded up into Cardiff General still struggling a bit from the signal check at Newtown, through the platform and take the left-hand signal for the Curve. Our relief was waiting opposite Canton shed on the Penarth Curve, they would take the train to Barry. We come to a stand, the relief climbs up, we get down after passing a few comments and make our way to the station to travel home.

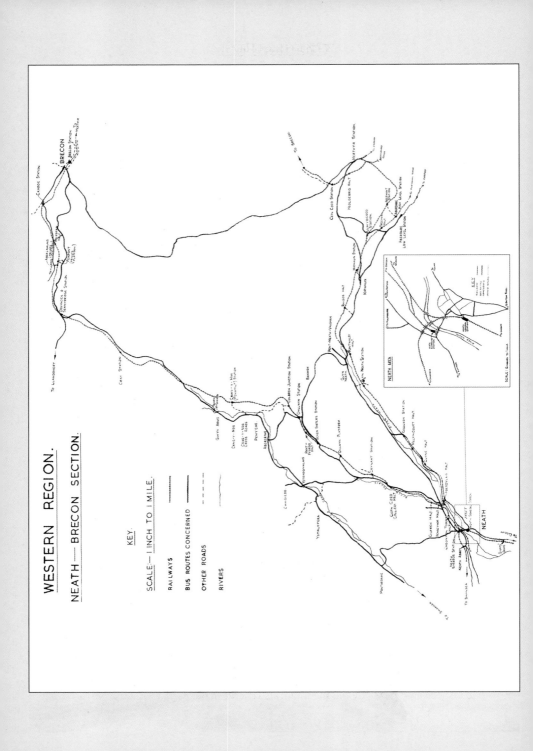

Chapter Four

Neath & Brecon Duties

A typical duty at the N&B shed would be as follows. The driver would book on duty one hour and the fireman would book on 45 minutes before leaving shed. After looking at the duty sheet for the day which indicated the allotted number of your locomotive, you would start to prepare your engine. First you would climb onto the footplate and inspect the level of water in the boiler, usually about halfway up the gauge glass, which was mounted on the front of the boiler, then check your steam pressure possibly 50 lb. The fire would already have been lit by the firelighter and he would also have paid attention to the water levels in the boiler.

Looking into the firebox you would probably find the fire around the back end of the box. Making sure the damper was open you would then get out the pricker bar and push the fire all over the grate area, then add about eight shovels of coal over the burning grate to start building your fire up, also putting the blower on a little to excite the fire. Initially you would then check your tank water cock to see it was coming out of the top cock meaning that your tanks were at least ¾ full.

Next you checked your footplate tools: shovel, bar, pricker, bucket, brush, pep pipe, pick, gauge glass spanners, spare gauge glass with rubbers. Then, before climbing down off the footplate, you would pull front and rear sand levers which would allow sand to run onto the rails. You would look to see that there were four mounds of sand on the rail, adjacent to each sand pipe; if not you had problems, wet sand in the sand box. This meant you would have to empty the sand box of wet sand and refill it with dry sand, also topping up the three other boxes with sand.

Then came checking the smokebox, the blower had already been increased so making it safe to open the smokebox. On inspection you would check for any damp patches in the fly ash, if so you would indicate this to the driver, also if an area around a pipe was clear of ash this sometimes would indicate that steam was blowing in that area. It was necessary also to check for blows from the tubes, this would show as bubbles and drips coming from around the tubes, this would also be reported to the driver, and all excessive ash would be shovelled out.

The lamps would then be collected from the stores, the paraffin levels checked and the glasses cleaned, making sure that the red slide glass was in its holder. If you did not have a full complement of tools on the footplate you would probably have to rob other engines to make up your kit.

Climbing back up onto the footplate, steam pressure would possibly be about 80 lb. by now, check the fire and in areas where needed add a few shovels of coal. Also at this time pull the gauge glass blow-down lever to ascertain if the water still remained at half a glass.

Then it would be up onto the coal bunker with the brush and pick to trim the bunker and brush all the coal from the top of the cab, which had been deposited there by the coalman. At this time the driver would be going about his duties, oiling and checking the locomotive, he would have put a 'Not to be Moved' sign on the engine before going underneath to oil. He would also check the ash pan to see if it had been cleared of ash by the shedman, also checking the firebars at the same time.

Pannier tank No. 9662 waits to leave Neath (Low Level) with the 8.25 am to Brecon on 14th
January, 1961.   *C.M. & J.M. Bentley*

0-6-0PT No. 9748 runs through Neath (Low Level) with a coal train bound for Jersey Marine
yards.   *Norman Jones*

The N&B yard showing the new sidings (*far left*), coal stage (*centre*) and goods shed (*centre right*).
W. Scaplehorn

The coal stage is on the left with the Cadoxton Brewery top left. The expanse of the N&B yard is in the centre foreground. *W. Scaplehorn*

The top end of Neath N&B yard with the N&B Yard signal box in the middle distance and the shunters' cabin in the centre foreground. The Tennant Canal can be seen on the right.

W. Scaplehorn

Neath Yard signal box, the first branch token was picked up here.   *Bill Davies*

C. W. PO CHULAT WESTERN RAILWAY.
MN

H. WILLIAMS.
Divisional Superintendent.

Telegrams:
DIVISIONAL, GREAT WESTERN
SWANSEA.

Telephone :
SWANSEA 2924. Exam. N. 6

reference:

DIVISIONAL SUPERINTENDENT'S OFFICE,
SWANSEA.

19th. November, 1946.

Please quote this reference :

SE.52

Memorandum to:- Woman Grade 1 Porter
Cilfrew.

In view of the change in the labour
situation following the end of the war and
the demobilisation of the Forces, the time has
arrived when it is necessary to terminate your
employment with the Company, and I have to
inform you that your services will not be
required after 30th instant.

The Company greatly appreciate the
splendid work performed by the large number of
women who have undertaken duty in the railway
service in the national interest during and
since the war, and I should like to express to
you the Company's thanks for the services which
you have rendered.

ASSISTANT

During World War II many women worked on the railway doing jobs that had previously been held by men. This letter terminates a women grade 1 porter's employment at Cilfrew little more than a year after hostilities ceased.

A pannier tank on a Neath-bound passenger train runs through Cilfrew passing loop. Another pannier tank with a train of pools waits opposite the signal box and waits for the token to work on to Crynant.   *David Lawrence*

Cefn Coed colliery *circa* 1955 with the N&B lines running through the middle of the complex.
                                                                                        Neath Museum

About 15 minutes before going off shed the steam pressure had probably risen to about 150 lb. and it was now time to test the water injectors to see if they were picking up, also filling the boiler, the second injector would also be checked and put off as soon as it was found okay. The fire would again be looked at and a few more shovels put around the box in areas that had burnt through. If the steam pressure was now getting to a better condition, possibly 180 lb., the firehole door would be left open and the blower turned down to its minimum and the engine was left to simmer. By this time the driver would have finished oiling and shouted up to the fireman on the footplate to move her up to the water column to top up the tanks. The driver would have probably gone back to the shed to put his prep kit in his locker and you were left to top up the tanks which did not take too long because they would probably be over ¾ full, filled by the shed staff.

When the driver returned the last job was usually cleaning the cab, an oily bit of waste was passed over all the pipework followed by a clean wipe, the fireman would do his side and the driver would do his area. The fireman would sweep up the footplate and wash down with the pep pipe and water the coal, also fill the bucket with water for a wash.

If it was now time to leave shed, we would drop down to the shed points, turn ourselves out towards the main line and wait at the signal. The fireman usually went to the lineside phone by the shed staff cabin and made contact with the signalman, saying something like 'Hello Bobby, 10.10 Onllwyn, ready to leave shed'. By the time you climbed back onto the footplate the points had come over and the signal dropped 'off'.

We would then make our way to the N&B yard and join the train, 60 pools (empty wagons), two brake vans, which was our load for Onllwyn, two locomotives, one in front and one in the rear (banker). The train engine (front locomotive) would probably drop into the new siding with his brakevan, pull out 60 empties onto the branch, when he was clear of the bottom points, the rear engine would blow three on his whistle for the front locomotive to stop, and the bank engine and brakevan would move onto the rear of the train and couple up. The enginemen would then wait for the road, when the signal came 'off' they would exchange two crows on the whistle and away at 10.10 to Onllwyn.

When a train was assisted in rear by a bank engine, the train engine driver would be shown the single line token, after which it would be carried by the bank engine. Once we left Neath yard we started to fire the engine continuously, four shovels in the corners, then four shovels around the sides of the box and this would go on continually until we slowed down for Cilfrew loop where we would wait for a down train. The injector would go on as soon as the water dropped in the glass and would stay on; if she started to blow off you would put the second injector on to keep a healthy level in the boiler.

Once the board dropped 'off' for Crynant the same procedure would be adopted, two whistles crows and away out of Cilfrew loop, over the river bridge and onto the climb, past Cefn Coed Colliery and Cefn Coed Colliery Halt, over the main road bridge and into Crynant loop. By this time the water tanks had gone down to half and water was needed. The front engine would take charge of the train, the rear locomotive shut down, and the train engine would stop for water. By this time the locomotive was blowing off steam and the flap had to be dropped and the injector

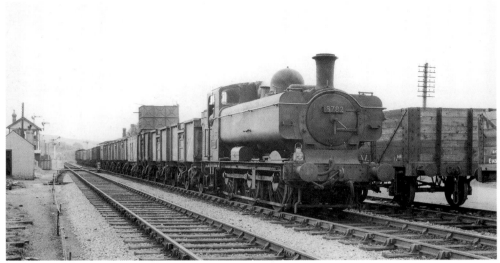

Pannier tank No. 8782 with a train of pools at Crynant passing loop waiting for a down train to pass after taking water.   *Hugh Davies*

Up and down coal trains pass at Crynant. The pannier tank on the left has been filled to overflowing from the water tank. Signalman Jim Cardonnel stands ready with the token.
                                                                                        Neath Antiquarians

With snow on the ground a pannier tank waits in the loop at Ynysdawley as another pannier tank passes with a passenger train bound for Neath. *W. Scaplehorn*

An up Brecon passenger train waits to leave Seven Sisters in 1960. *R.K. Blencowe*

Onllwyn south sidings in the snow with another pannier tank at work. The line to the right goes to Onllwyn colliery yard.   W. *Scaplehorn*

A winter scene at Onllwyn station. A pannier tank with a brake van stands behind the signal box waiting to pick up mineral wagons from the south sidings. In the up platform another pannier tank waits with a passenger train bound for Brecon.   W. *Scaplehorn*

Onllwyn permanent way gang with the colliery in the background *circa* 1950s. *Gerald Williams*

The permanent way gang pose for this picture at the foot of the steps of Onllwyn signal box *circa* 1950s. *Gerald Williams*

A pannier tank with a train of overflow (in reserve) empty wagons at Colbren storage sidings, with Onllwyn colliery in the background.   *N.C. Simmons*

A pannier tank on an up Brecon passenger train takes water at Colbren in 1960. Passenger train locomotives took water at Crynant and Colbren.   *R.K. Blencowe*

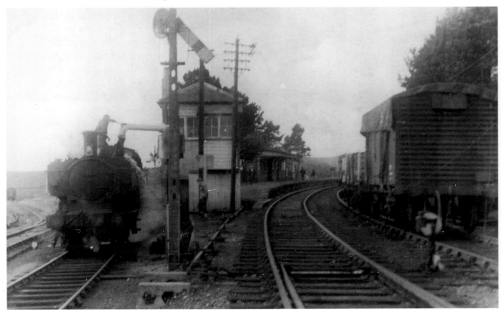

worked so as not to over fill the boiler or the engine would prime, 'blow water from the stack', and the driver would have something to say about that.

When the front engine had topped his tanks he would indicate with a whistle and the banker would take charge of the train as far as the water column and the front engine would shut down. When we lined up for the water tank the fireman would jump up on top of the tanks, put the bag in the filler hole and pull the chain to release the water from the tank. When the tank was full one side we would have to wait for the tank to level itself by cutting down the pressure until the tanks were full, bag out, tank filler top on, back on the footplate, check the fire and boiler. By this time the down train had passed which was a coal train, the driver was 'running them' smoke coming off the pinned-down brakes on the coal wagons, the smell of hot metal with brake blocks rubbing against wheel metals left the train shrouded in a blue haze, a combination of dust and metal smoke coming from the train, at the rear the brake van with handbrake on, making the train complete.

Once the starting signal had been lowered the footplate staff exchanged whistles two crows and away, hopefully all the way to Onllwyn, sometimes we would also have to stop at Ynysdawley loop to pass a train, but today we had a clear run. After leaving Crynant we passed Crynant New Colliery, into Dillwyn Colliery, pass the old Brynteg Colliery, round the bend in Ynysdawley loop, signals 'off', rear engine changing token, firing continues, injector on and forgotten about, coal going in the firebox, four in the corners, short break, four shovels around the sides of the box, short spell, four shovels in the corners, and on it goes all the way to Onllwyn.

Once we left Ynysdawley loop it was over the notorious Nanthir stream into Seven Sisters station, past Seven Sisters Colliery through Pantyffordd Halt passing the stop board for all down trains, into Onllwyn where the train engine took over the train to stop for water at Onllwyn station, the same procedure was now adopted as at Crynant. The train engine would now pull the empty coal wagons over the colliery top point and push them into the colliery where the colliery locomotive would take over. By this time the banking engine would have dropped down onto the coal wagons bound for Neath yard, the guard had started taking the tally (names of all the wagon labels) and would finally come to the engine and tell the driver how many he had on and what the load was, the maximum for the bank was 33 wagons of coal for Group A to C engines.

After leaving the colliery transfer siding we would pull out onto the branch with the guard putting down brakes on the wagons with his brake stick until the driver felt he had enough down and blew two on the whistle. The guard would then drop his brakevan on to the train after which the driver eased down to the stop board, stopped the train, and then pulled away full regulator. If he had too many brakes down he would be unable to pull away, so you will understand that there was a great deal of skill in this practice. The fireman by this time had reversed the dampers* and was cutting down the shovelling because the box was looking quite healthy and would only put coal on where it was needed. He had, before departure, picked up the token from the signalman and shown it to the driver, he could now relax to some extent. Some drivers, if they had the road and worked the regulator well, could run the train all the way

---

* This was the lever in the cab floor of the engine, one for the front ashpan door and the other for the rear ashpan door; you would not open the front one when going forward or the back one when going backwards because the draft would blow the fire out of the firehole door and onto the footplate with the obvious consequences.

without too much regulator; down coal trains were usually given the road with a full load for Neath yard. After changing tokens at Ynysdawley, Crynant, Cilfrew and Cadoxton, the train terminated at Neath yard.

When finally stopped at Neath yard the engine would be uncoupled and leave the train on the bank, the fireman would examine his fire and deposit any clinker he found. The shunter, together with his brakesman, would gravitate the wagons into their respective sidings for forward transit. The brakevan was then dropped down into the sidings ready for the next trip. The locomotive would now go into the new siding to pick up 33 pools for his second trip to Crynant, this time without assistance at the rear, just a single load. This gives you some idea of a typical trip up the branch.

When the train reached Neath the fireman had already made the tea, the teacan boiled on the fire with a specially made can-iron which would allow the can to be hung inside the firehole door. It took about 10 seconds to boil, if you did not have a can iron you would use the shovel. At Neath you would probably have about half an hour to eat your food, sometimes you would have to eat your food on the move. The favourite was a tin of beans which had two holes punched in the top, behind a hot pipe. Some drivers had their tea in a bottle which was put behind the hot pipes and would warm gently over half a shift and could be drunk when needed.

12.40 pm Neath N&B to Swansea St Thomas

When working the 12.40 Neath N&B to Swansea, St Thomas, we would take 33 pools from Neath N&B yard or sometimes Cadoxton 'Bone Yard' (next to the cemetery), working them to Colbren. The firing procedure was the same as the 10.10 duty only missing out on water at Onllwyn but taking it at Colbren instead. The 12.40 would now spend about an hour at Colbren, shunt the yard, by this time the 10.40 goods from Brecon had arrived which was allocated 30 minutes shunting at this point. We would then take water, join our train which was standing in the down platform ready for the descent into the Swansea Valley.

When arriving at the colliery at Abercrave and if we were dropping empties off, we would cut off and leave the train on the branch above the inward colliery point and pin half the brakes down. The engine would then drop forward clear of the points, the guard would open the ground frame and gravitate the empties into the colliery. The guard would not object if the fireman helped him with this movement because the incline at this point was severe, and he always carried an extra brake stick.

After this movement was over the point was reset for the branch and locked and the token returned to the driver, the guard would gravitate his van onto the rest of the train which would now drop down to the outward ground frame. The guard would pin brakes down and the locomotive would uncouple and drop clear of the ground frame points, the token again would have to be used to release the points for the outward colliery roads. The engine would then pick up the loaded coal wagons and pull out onto the branch. When clear of the points the guard would pin a number of brakes down and reverse the colliery points, the locomotive and coal wagons would rejoin the rest of the train on the branch. From this point the guard would adjust the brakes on the train until the driver was happy, when he would blow two on his whistle and the guard would jump on his brakevan and give the tip to the driver, right away.

The next stop would be Penrhos Brick Works if we had brought empty palbrick wagons from Colbren for this shunt and the same procedure as at Abercrave would be adopted here. The next stop was Varteg Colliery, the remaining empties would again be gravitated in at the top end points and coal taken out at the outward ground frame. This colliery was smaller than Abercrave and took less traffic, the Abercrave Colliery, also known as the International Colliery, closed in 1967. Varteg closed in 1965 and Penrhos Brick Works in 1958.

In later years, after the Ynis-y-Geinon Jn section closed in February 1967, the remaining traffic from this branch, Abercrave Colliery only, was worked up the line to Colbren. The load for one engine was 12 loaded wagons and most times the train made two trips from Colbren to the Abercrave branch to clear the traffic.

When I worked the branch, after leaving Varteg we would run down the branch until we came to Ynis-y-Geinon Jn (junction for Gurnos LMS) and change our token with the signalman and receive a new token to Ynis-y-Geinon Sidings. But first we would shunt at Ynis-y-Geinon Yard to make up our load for Swansea Docks. We would change tokens at Pontardawe, Glais Jn, at this point we would take the Llansamlet, Six Pit branch, coming onto the double track section at Six Pit where we handed in the token. (After Six Pit box closed in 1963, the token would be surrended at Upper Bank.)

After leaving Upper Bank we progressed with our train through St Thomas yard, by this time it had got dark and I can always remember the old 'Jinty' tank simmering in the sidings waiting for work. We would then pass Port Tennant yards and Swansea East Dock loco shed and into Burrows yard sidings where we would berth our train. We would then pick up the brakevan and propel into the Violet Siding in the Swansea Docks to pick up pools, empty wagons for the N&B collieries.

By this time the fire needed attention, it had started to deteriorate (clinkering up), time had to be given here to cleaning the fire with the pricker and bar, pulling the clinker to the rear of the box. If it was excessive it had to come out and the fire rebuilt.

After leaving the dock with 60 pools it was flat out all the way to Jersey Marine Jn, where the line rose to Neath Abbey before we ran into the low level platform. Sometimes the fire would become dirty by this point and we had to assist the steam pressure problem with the use of the blower. The operation at this point would be in compliance with the N&B shunter either pulling over to Neath Jn and propelling the pools into the new sidings or sometimes going on to the 'Bone Yard' at Cadoxton, picking up the shunter on the way.

Finally we would put the brakevan into the sidings and engine to shed, leaving it on the coal stage, and walk back to the shed to book off.

Percy Bate with the Colbren permanent way motor trolley outside Craig-y-Nos signal box *circa* 1950s. *Percy Bate*

The 4.10 pm from Neath leaves Craig-y-Nos on 27th January, 1962. After leaving Craig-y-Nos you went onto the windswept section of the Bwlch mountain, and on bad days you had to huddle up in the confines of the cab. *Tudor Watkins*

4.10 pm to Brecon

After taking up my appointment in 1955 as junior fireman at Neath & Brecon shed, I was allocated a vacancy in the pilot link. This link had five duties, two at Neath N&B yard and three turns at Neath Junction (Klondyke), the third turn being a night shift with an amount of local tripping between the junction and Neath General. When working the morning and afternoon turns I was frequently moved into the train links due to a shortage of firemen and the cleaners used to work the pilot turns.

After approximately six weeks at the depot, I was taken off the yard pilot when the fireman on the 4.10 pm to Brecon did not turn up for duty. The shed cleaner relieved me and informed me that I had to report to the shed to prepare the engine for this turn. On arrival at the depot a cleaner had already started to prepare the engine No. 7701 and when climbing onto the footplate I noticed that the driver on this duty was Ben Mathias, a very dry person who never spoke much to his fireman, kept himself very much to himself, and was reputed to be a very rough driver.

We eventually presented our engine to the signalman and he let us out of the shed to the low level station to join our coaches which had been shunted there by the N&B yard pilot ready for our arrival. When we backed on and I had coupled up, I noticed that we had a horse box next to the engine. Looking into the vehicle I observed that it was empty, and on enquiring, the guard told me it was for a special shunt at Sennybridge and was to be left there for livestock.

When the driver had blown up the vacuum we found that we could not hold our pressure, and after a look around by the examiner who always met this train, a defective vacuum pipe was located on the horse box and had to be changed. After the repair we again blew up pressure and our two coaches and a horse box left the station five minutes late, so look out, fireman, I was obviously in for a rough time.

The fire at this stage was low and fed in a saucer pattern, this was the usual type of fire for bank work with a pannier, and always had good results. After leaving the station the driver opened up full regulator and after picking up the token from the yard box which made my hand sting, we thundered through the yard and up the bank to Cadoxton. By the time we approached the Cadoxton box we were really moving, and although I had plenty of token changing on mineral train working, I had never before changed it at such a fast speed. I positioned my token ready for the change, and on impact I grabbed my token, Cadoxton to Cilfrew, but also hung onto the other one, partly pulling the signalman out of his token platform.

The signalman then released my token and it struck the horse box and signal box wall and then fell into the six foot; I looked back and saw the signalman hanging over the token platform rail and uttering a strange warlike cry.

Our next stop was Crynant, apart from changing tokens at Cilfrew. When we rounded the curve at Cilfrew, I noticed the starter was on and the signalman was standing outside his box with a red flag unfurled. I thought the worst. The driver obviously knew something was amiss, but said nothing. We pulled up at the box and the signalman approached the engine and said that the signalman had contacted him from Cadoxton, and said that the fireman had nearly pulled his arm out of its socket by holding onto the token, and that he thought we were going too fast anyway. The driver said nothing, and after passing orders to slow down when changing tokens, the signalman told us to proceed and handed the

'8750' class 0-6-0PT No. 3611 has just arrived at Brecon (Free Street) with the 8.25 am from Neath on 11th September, 1951.   *H.C. Casserley*

A small turntable was provided at Free Street station. '4575' class 2-6-2T No. 5516 is being turned in this July 1947 scene. Engines were turned to even out the wear on wheel flanges.
D.B. Clayton

Brecon goods yard from the water tower showing the low and high level sidings in 1962.

Ron Gell

A view from Brecon shed water tower looking towards the former Mid-Wales Railway terminus of Watton. This station closed in 1871 when the Brecon & Merthyr Railway's Free Street station opened. The former station continued in use as a goods station until closure. *Ron Gell*

A view across the shed yard at Brecon with three ex-GWR '2251' class 0-6-0s and an Ivatt 2-6-0, referred to as a 'Mickey Mouse' by enginemen, in 1962.   *Ron Gell*

Brecon engine shed looks in a rather forlorn state, it having closed in December 1962. Pannier tank No. 9676 waits to depart with a train from the goods shed on 3rd September, 1963. To the right is Watton station, the former Mid-Wales Railway terminus.   *B.J. Ashworth*

token to the driver who looked at me with a grin on his face. We left Cilfrew at a fast rate and stopped at Crynant where the guard came up to the engine for a quick word, what had happened? I told him, and he left with a grin on his face.

We were now about eight minutes late and we literally flew to Colbren, stopping only at Seven Sisters and Onllwyn. We topped our tanks at Colbren, this filling usually lasted us until we got back to Sennybridge on the return journey. If we were low at Brecon we had to take our engine to Brecon shed as there was no water column at the station. After leaving Colbren it was the final ascent to the Bwlch and then next stop Sennybridge. Putting off the horse box in the sidings cost us a further five minutes, and apparently was an unusual move on this working. We stopped at Aberbran and Cradoc, then over the viaduct into Brecon station five minutes late. We then ran around our coaches and crossed over to the back of the down platform, where we had about an ½ hour lay-over, our return time was 6.20 pm from Brecon.

When we returned to Neath that evening the signalman at Cadoxton signal box would not take the token from me and I had to drop it into the six foot. He did put the Neath yard token up for me to take but was not happy; I did say sorry. Well, you can't blame him, probably still smarting from his previous encounter. This story soon got around the shed and for the next few weeks everybody was demonstrating how a token should be changed. And the rumour goes that the signalman's arm was never the same again, and that it was six inches longer.

The Afternoon Glyncorrwg (1955)

While working at the Neath & Brecon shed I was seconded for outstation work at Glyncorrwg. This work was usually covered by Duffryn Yard (Port Talbot) men but due to staff shortages we were asked to cover this duty. Stan Jones the shed master called me in and said that there was a staff problem at Duffryn Yard and would I and a driver from the N&B cover work at Glyncorrwg. Being on the Pilots at the time I jumped at the idea to break the monotony of shunting work. The driver was a passed fireman and had knowledge of the duty involved.

The branch opened in 1863 as the South Wales Mineral Railway from Briton Ferry to North Rhondda Colliery. A passenger service was run between Cymmer and Glyncorrwg between March 1918 and 22nd September, 1930. Four trains each way were run with extras on Saturdays. The GWR put on a bus service between these points in 1930. After withdrawal of the passenger service, a workmen's service from Cymmer Corrwg to the colleries survived until 1958, after which date they only ran between Glyncorrwg and the North Rhondda Halt. New colliery passenger stock was introduced in 1954 replacing old type clerestory stock. In 1963 the service was further cut back to the South Pit Halt and finally withdrawn from 30th October, 1964. The branch closed in 1970.

So on the Monday we travelled on the 2.25 pm bus from Neath to Cymmer and then transferred onto the Glyncorrwg bus for the 15 minute journey to the village. There the morning men were walking to meet us, they got on the 3.10 pm bus to travel to Duffryn Yard while we made our way to the station yard and climbed aboard our '96XX' class pannier tank. I checked the water and fire and the coal in the bunker to see if it needed trimming but everything was satisfactory.

The driver walked around the engine and I went into the cabin to ask how much time we had before they needed us for the colliery. The shunter advised me that there was a train of empties on its way from Cymmer, we would take over this train in the station allowing the train engine to return with a coal train. I reported to my mate who was putting a drop of oil around, I climbed up onto the footplate and started building up my fire for the incline to North Rhondda.

Eventually the train of 40 empties arrived and stopped in the station with the engine blowing off. The shunter uncoupled the locomotive, the signalman closed the gates and gave us the road to come out of the sidings onto the bank by the small engine shed. The train engine came out to meet us and then dropped back down the loop to pick up his brake van from the rear of the train and put ours on and then dropped down to the bottom ground frame to pick up his coal train to return to Cymmer.

We then backed onto the empties, by this time the steam had come around nicely and started to blow off. I put the injector on to fill the boiler and keep the engine quiet because we were outside the box. We eventually got the road, a tip from the guard, gates closed again, board drops 'off' and we climb out of the station onto the bank for the climb to South and North Rhondda, just over a mile away. My mate told me to put the blower on a bit as the engine was cold; although the boiler pressure was on the mark, the engine had been standing in the yard for an hour and needed that extra enticement for the immediate climb to the colliery. The ruling gradient here was as steep as 1 in 22!

We pounded up towards the colliery, the steam dropped back and my mate increased the blower to hold our pressure. I started firing like the N&B pattern around the box leaving the middle open all the way to South Rhondda. My mate had reduced the blower pressure because the blast had now kicked in and the steam pressure was coming around nicely but the boiler had dropped to half. My mate told me to put the injector on when she blew off and I did just that; we were now passing the small colliers' platform at South Pit and really pounding into the bank. The colliery was sandwiched between the two mountains and the blast from the engine was sounding quite extensive for a small engine. We were passing the main screens now at South Pit and well into the climb, still firing, steam dropping back with the injector on but still healthy and water level up to three-quarters. I turned the injector off, steam now picks up and soon blew off, injector on again, we were now nearing the colliery platform at North Rhondda Colliery and onto the final leg of our journey. We finally arrived at North Rhondda Colliery and stopped when the guard gave us the tip. He would then uncouple the brakevan and drop it clear of the points and then the shunter would turn the point for the south colliery and give us the tip to push in. When you took the steam brake off the train would move very quickly into the sidings and the driver would have to keep them well under control with the brake, also the colliery shunter would drop brakes on the wagons. When clear of the branch we would stop and our shunter would cut off and put further brakes down.

We would then regain the branch and couple up to our brakevan, propelling it down the incline towards South Pit and onwards to Glyncorrwg Yard blowing our whistle to the signalman for the gates and the signal for the yard. By the time we got to the crossing everything would be ready to put our brakevan behind our train for Margam to be worked later on in the turn of duty.

The next duty at Glyncorrwg was the colliers' passenger trip, we would pick up the old wooden seat coaches in the platform spur and propel them from the platform with the guard sitting in the front end of the leading coach which was fitted with an observation window and a bell, the driver remaining on the footplate to control the train. We then ran to the North Rhondda platform and waited for the colliers, after which we would drop down the incline to the South Rhondda platform to pick up the colliers there. We then proceeded to Glyncorrwg platform, where some of the colliers would get off, and the guard would give us the tip and we would make our way to Cymmer Corrwg platform at Cymmer passing the old Nantewleth Colliery on the way.

On arrival at Cymmer Corrwg the colliers would de-train and the guard would check all the doors and return to the leading coach and give us the tip to proceed. We would propel our coaches back up the branch to Glyncorrwg where we would stable the coaches in the platform sidings.

Our final duty was to work a train to Margam at 7 pm after the colliery needs had been attended to; we would take water topping our tanks at the water tank outside the old engine shed and light the engine lamps. The engine would then drop down to the bottom ground frame, the shunter would turn us into the sidings while the guard was checking the train. The shunter would remain on the engine as he lived between Glyncorrwg and Nantewleth Colliery and we would slow down to drop him off.

When the guard had checked the train he would start putting a few brakes down, we would pull out of the sidings, the driver would blow two on the whistle and we would pull down to the stop board. The guard would reset the ground frame for the branch and walk to the locomotive and give the driver the staff which he had obtained from the signalman. He would then rejoin his brakevan and give us the tip 'right away', we would then make our way down the grade to Cymmer through Cymmer Corrwg platform, over the large steel viaduct into Cymmer South Jn, into the Cymmer/Caerau tunnel (1,595 yards long) to the stop board at the top of Caerau bank. Here the guard would re-adjust the brakes and we would then proceed to Maesteg through the platform and again stop for the guard to adjust the brakes because the worst of the incline had now passed. From there we would pass the platform at Troedyrhiew Garth, through the platforms at Llangynwyd, sometimes we would get held up here for a passing train, then onto the paper mills and into Tondu yards, passing Tondu shed, and onto the Pyle branch through the platforms of Tondu station. It was getting dark now and we were on our way to Cefn Jn, into Kenfig Hill station, passing under the main line on Stormy bank and down the bank through Pyle station passing Pyle West loop signal box and into the long loops at Margam East. We would pass Margam Middle and into the down sidings, putting our train off here, then run engine and van to Port Talbot Yard where we would have relief with a Duffryn Yard set. The latter would then work home engine and van to Duffryn Yard through Aberavon station and then via the Tonygroes loop.

We would make our way to the General station at Port Talbot and catch a passenger train home to Neath and book off. This went on for three weeks until the staffing problem at Glyncorrwg was resolved. The N&B driver on this duty was Brian Morgan and this outstation work has been confirmed by Danny Counsell who was involved in supervisory work at the time.

This story is an outline of work carried out at Glyncorrwg and although there might be items that are not entirely accurate after 50 years this is the best I can remember of this duty.

I have been advised by retired Duffryn Yard men that their Glyncorrwg duties went something like this: 2.35 am Duffryn Yard 60 pools and banker work to Glyncorrwg, the train engine remaining at Glyncorrwg to work the early workmen's train and then serviced the collieries at South and North Rhondda. The banker worked a coal train back to Duffryn Yard and then banked the 6.10 am Duffryn Yard to Cymmer.

The Glyncorrwg outstation men would relieve the 2.35 am set at 8.00 am and these men would catch the 8.10 am bus from Glyncorrwg to Port Talbot. The outstation men would then work the outstation duty until 4.00 pm. An afternoon set of Duffryn Yard men would then travel by bus to Glyncorrwg to relieve the day set, they would work the afternoon workmen's train and then return with a coal train for Margam downside, then engine/van to Duffryn Yard. This is the duty I covered for three weeks, as described above.

There was also a 6.10 am engine and banker that worked empties to Glyncorrwg from Duffryn Yard and returned with coal for Margam.

Glyncorrwg Workmen's Train Workings

am	
5.40	Glyncorrwg (ECS)
5.48	Cymmer Corrwg (arrive)
6.00	Cymmer Corrwg (depart) Workmen's train
6.15	Glyncorrwg
6.25	North Rhondda (arrive)
7.00	North Rhondda (depart ECS)
7.10	Glyncorrwg (put coaches into sidings)

pm	
2.15	Glyncorrwg
2.24	North Rhondda Halt (arrive)
2.53	North Rhondda Halt (depart)
3.03	Glyncorrwg (arrive)
3.10	Glyncorrwg (depart)
3.14	South Pit Halt (arrive)
3.20	South Pit Halt (depart)
3.28	Glyncorrwg
3.37	Cymmer Corrwg (arrive)
3.44	Cymmer Corrwg (depart (ECS)
3.52	Glyncorrwg (stable coaches)

Note: ECS = Empty coaching stock

Glyncorrwyg yard *circa* 1912. South Wales Mineral Railway 0-6-0ST No. 8 had a long and interesting history. She was built by the Avonside Engine Co. to broad gauge for the South Devon Railway and was named *Achilles*. She was later regauged and became GWR No. 1324 and was subsequently purchased by the SWMR in April 1905. On returning to GWR stock at the Grouping the engine was renumbered 818 and continued in service until 1932.   *Gerald Williams Collection*

Freight Traffic on the Neath & Brecon

The Neath & Brecon line between Neath and Onllwyn, and from Colbren to Ynys-y-Geinon formed one of the busiest freight single lines in South Wales, mostly coal traffic, but other freight traffic included pit props from Neath Yard and the saw mills at Devynock, military traffic to Brecon and Devynock, and household coal, to Craig-y-Nos, Devynock, Crynant and Colbren.

Unwashed coal from collieries at Crynant, Dillwyn and Seven Sisters went to Onllwyn for washing and screening; trains conveyed a maximum of 12 loaded wagons because of the gradients. Washed coal went directly to Neath N&B yard, empties going from there to the collieries. The 9.10 Duty worked pit props from Neath Yard.

When the Ynys-y-Geinon branch closed at the Ynys-y-Geinon end the N&B based locomotives used to work the coal from Abercrave Colliery to Colbren, and when all the traffic was shunted at Colbren this would be worked to Neath N&B Yard. In the years 1955 to 1960 all of the coal traffic went into Neath N&B Yard but from 1960 block trains of coal used to run through to Swansea Docks for shipment.

Up until 1962 all coal trains were worked by pannier tanks, but after 1962, '42XX' class engines were tested on the line and numbers included were 4275 (ex-Severn Tunnel), 4252 (ex-Neath), 7248 (from Landore). When No. 7248 was derailed at Seven Sisters it was decided to withdraw this type of locomotive ('72XX') from the branch.

Neath men worked the stone trains from Craig-y-Nos on a control turn (run when required) usually once a week, the stone traffic worked via Neath Jn to Llanwern Steel Works.

WEEKDAYS

BRECON TO NEATH (RIVERSIDE)

DOUBLE LINE—Neath (Riverside) to Neath Yard Signal Box.
SINGLE LINE—Worked by Electric Train Token, Neath Yard Signal Box to Brecon Station Signal Box.

Sections	Crossing Stations	Sections	Crossing Station
Neath Yard Signal Box and Cadoxton	Cadoxton **a**	Ynisdawley and Onllwyn	Onllwyn
Cadoxton and Cilfrew	Cilfrew	Onllwyn and Colbren Junction	Onllwyn
Cilfrew and Crynant	Crynant	Colbren Jct. and Devynock and Sennybridge	Devynock and Sennybridge
Crynant and Ynisdawley	Ynisdawley	Devynock and Sennybridge and Brecon	Brecon Station Signal Box

a—Two Passenger Trains must not cross at Cadoxton, but an Up Passenger Train and a Down Freight Train may do so, the Freight Train to run into the Loop and be clear before the Passenger Train is accepted from Neath Yard.
Intermediate Token Instruments are provided at Cefn Coed Colliery Sidings and Onllwyn Goods Loop to enable trains to pass over the Main Line whilst a train or engine is in the Sidings or Loop.

DOWN

Mileage from Brecon M	C		Ruling Gradient from previous place mentioned 1 in		B Workmen (Advertised Second Class only)		B (Saturdays and School Holidays excepted)	B SO		B		B SO (Advertised Second Class only)		B SX Workmen (Advertised Second Class only)	B Passenger and Mail
					am		am	am		am		PM		PM	PM
	23	**BRECON** .. .. ..dep	416 R	..		..		8 5	..	11 0	..	..	..		6 20
2	77½	Cradoc	60 R					8 11		11 6					6 26
5	7	Aberbran Halt	60 F	..		..		8 16	..	11 12	..		..		6 32
9	1½	Devynock and Sennybridge arr	60 R					8 25		11 20					6 40
		.. ..dep	..	..		..		8 27	..	11 23	..		..		6 43
12	43¾	Cray	50 R					8 36		11 32					6 52
19	9¾	Craig-y-nos .. ..dep	51 R	..		..		8 51	..	11c49	..		..		7 8
22	33½	**COLBREN JUNCTION** arr	50 F					8 58		11 56					7 15
		.. ..dep	..	..	6 35	..	8 10	9 0	..	11 58	..	2 30	..	3 0	7 17
23	20	Onllwyn .. ..arr	70 F		6 38		..	9X 2		12X 0				3 2	
		.. ..dep	..	..	6X45	..	8 13	9 8	..	12 5	..	2 33	..	3 5	7 20
23	70	Pantyffordd Halt	57 F		6 48		8 16	9 11		12 8		2 36		3 8	7 23
24	69¾	Seven Sisters	57 F	..	6 52	..	8 19	9 14	..	12 11	..	2 39	..	3 12	7 27
25	33½	Ynisdawley ....dep	57 F		6 53		8 20	9 15		12 12		2 40		3 13	7 28
25	79¾	Dillwyn Platform .. ..dep	57 F	..	6 55	..	..	9 17	..	12 14	..	2 42	..	3c16	..
28	2¾	Crynant ....arr	160 F												
		.. ..dep	..	..	7X 1	..	8 27	9 22	..	12 20	..	2 47	..	3 22	7 35
29	49¾	Cefn Coed Colliery Halt	60 F		7 5		8 31	9 26		12 24		2 51		3 26	
31	16¾	Cilfrew Loop .. .. arr	60 F	..	..	..	8 35	..	..	..	..	..	..	..	..
		..........dep	..				8X38							3 30	7 43
31	38¾	Cilfrew Halt dep	74 F	..	7 11	..	8 39	9 31	..	12 30	..	2 57	..	3e34	7 45
32	14	Penscynor Halt	67 F		7 14		8 43	9 35		12 34		3 1		3 38	7 49
32	45	Cadoxton Terrace Halt ..dep	67 F	..	7 17	..	8 45	9 37	..	12 36	..	3 3	..	3 40	7 51
33	43	**NEATH (RIVERSIDE)** arr	L		7 20		8 48	9 40		12 39		3 6		3 43	7 54

UP

Mile Post Mileage Z M	C		Ruling Gradient from previous place mentioned 1 in		B Workmen		B	B SO		B		B SO		B SX	
					am		am	am		PM		PM		PM	
		NEATH (RIVERSIDE) dep	L	..	6 0	..	8 25	11 25	..	4 10	..	9 0	..	9 40	..
	78	Cadoxton Terrace Halt....dep	64 R		6 4		8 29	11 29		4 14		9c 5		9 44	
1	29	Penscynor Halt	67 R	..	6 7	..	8 32	11 32	..	4 17	..	9c 9	..	9 47	..
2	4¼	Cilfrew Halt ....dep	67 R		6 11		8 36	11 36		4 21		9c14		9 51	
2	26¼	Cilfrew Loop .. .. ..arr	74 R	..	..	..	8 37	..	..	..	..	..	..	..	..
		......dep			6 12		8X39	11 37		4 22		9 15		9 52	
4	30¼	Cefn Coed Colliery Halt	60 R	..	6 18	..	..	..	..	..	..	9 21	..	9 58	..
5	40¼	Crynant ....arr	60 R		6 21			11 45		4 30		9 24		10 1	
		.. ..dep	..	..	6 25	..	8 48	11 47	..	4 32	..	9 26	..	10 4	..
7	43¼	Dillwyn Platform ....dep	57 R		6 34					..				10e13	
8	9½	Ynisdawley .. .. ..dep	57 R	..	6 36	..	8 56	11 54	..	4 39	..	9 33	..	10 14	..
8	53¼	Seven Sisters	57 R		6 38		8 58	11 56		4 41		9N39		10 17	
9	39	Pantyffordd Halt..	57 R	..	6 42	..	9S02	12 0	..	4 45	..	9c44	..	10 21	..
10	23	Onllwyn ....arr	75 R		6 44		9X 4	12X 2		4 47		9 46		10 23	
		.. ..dep	..	..	6X47	..	9 5	12 4	..	4 48	..	9 47	..	10 24	..
11	9½	**COLBREN JUNCTION** arr	50 R		6 49		9 7	12 6		4 51		9 49		10 26	
		.. ..dep	..	..	Not advertised	..	9 9	12 7	..	4 53	..	..	..	..	..
14	33¼	Craig-y-nos ....dep	50 R				9e21	12 19		5 3					
20	79¼	Cray	51 F	..		..	9 39	12 37	..	5 21	..	Z Arrive 9.34 pm	..	..	..
24	41½	Devynock and Sennybridge arr	50 F				9 46	..		5 28					
		.. ..dep	..	..		..	9 48	12 46	..	5 30	..		..	..	..
28	36	Aberbran Halt	60 F				9 57	12 55		5 39					
30	45½	Cradoc	60 R	..	..	..	10c 4	1 2	..	5c46	..	..	..	..	..
33	13½	**BRECON** ....arr	416 F				10 9	1 7		5 51					

Z—7 chains to be added to give distances from Neath (Riverside)

The 1957 passenger working timetable for Neath to Brecon services.

Pannier tanks Nos. 9796 and 3706 prepare to leave Neath (Low Level). *F.K. Davies*

The final booked passenger train to Brecon, the 4.10 pm to Brecon on the last day of passenger services, 13th October, 1962. *Peter Jenkins*

Freight workings on the Neath & Brecon in September 1963

(MX)	Neath N&B	1.20	*am*	Onllwyn	2.26	*am*
	Onllwyn	3.40		N&B Yard	4.42	
	Neath N&B	5.20	am	Onllwyn	6.28	*am*
		Return working as required by control.				
	Neath N&B	6.20		Onllwyn	7.28	
	Onllwyn	8.35		N&B Yard	9.46	
(MX)	Neath N&B	6.40		Colbren	7.52	
	Colbren Yard	8.30		Abercrave	8.42	
	Abercrave	9.00		Colbren	9.19	
	Colbren	9.35		Neath N&B Yard	11.57	
(MO)	Neath	7.00		Colbren	8.12	
	Colbren Yard	8.30		Abercrave	8.42	
	Abercrave	9.00		Colbren	9.19	
	Colbren	9.35		Neath N&B Yard	11.57	
	Neath (N&B)	7.40		Onllwyn	9.10	
	Onllwyn	9.40		Seven Sisters	9.50/10.05	
	Onllwyn	10.18		Onllwyn Dep.	11.20	
	Neath N&B	12.22	*pm*			
	Neath N&B	8.25	*am* assisted	Onllwyn	10.48	
		('42XX' booked on this turn.)				
	Onllwyn	12.25	*pm*	Neath N&B	1.27	
	Neath N&B	10.20	*am*	Onllwyn	12.01	*pm*
	Onllwyn	1.05		Neath N&B	2.07	
(SX)	Neath N&B	12.30		Onllwyn	1.45	
	Onllwyn	2.50		Neath N&B	3.52	
(SX)	Neath N&B	2.15		Onllwyn	3.50	
		(Work engine and van to Crynant.)				
	Crynant	3.55		Neath N&B	4.21	
		(Alternate workings.)				
	Onllwyn	4.10		Dillwyn	4.29	
	Dillwyn	4.49		Onllwyn	5.03	
	Onllwyn	6.20		Neath N&B	7.22	
(SX)	Neath N&B	4.40		Onllwyn	6.13	
	Onllwyn	7.40		Neath N&B	8.42	
(SX)	Neath N&B	6.05		Onllwyn	7.30	
	Onllwyn	9.00		Neath N&B	10.02	
		('42XX' booked on this turn.)				
(SX)	Neath N&B	7.45		Onllwyn	8.51	
	Onllwyn	10.20		Neath	11.22	
(SX)	Neath N&B	9.05		Onllwyn	10.11	
	Onllwyn	11.40		Neath N&B	12.52	*am*
(SX)	Neath N&B	10.25	*pm*	Onllwyn	11.31	
	Onllwyn	1.15	*am*	Neath N&B	2.17	
(SX)	Neath N&B	11.45	*pm*	Onllwyn	12.56	*am*
(MX)	Onllwyn	2.35		Neath N&B	3.37	

Other N&B workings at N&B Shed

8.40 am Resolven Tripper ('Jazz').

11.45 pm N&B Yard work between there, Swansea Docks and Margam (SX).

Notes: MO - Mondays only, MX - Mondays excepted, SX - Saturdays excepted.

N&B locomotive allocation at this time: 12 '57XX' class 0-6-0PTS, two '42/52XX' class 2-8-0Ts.

The last passenger steam working over the N&B line from Neath was a double-headed railtour on 24th April, 1965. The train worked as a far as Colbren Junction and then continued its journey to Ynys-y-Geinon Junction and beyond. Pannier tank No. 9675 is seen on Neath (Court Sart) shed having received some special attention. *Norman Jones*

Court Sart shed staff pose in front of 0-6-0PT No. 4612, the other locomotive to work the special on 24th April, 1965. *Gerald Williams*

An English Electric type '3' Co-Co shunts at Crynant on the N&B line in 1964/65.

Tudor Watkins

English Electric type '3' No. D6926 with a train of pools at Onllwyn. To the left is the old inlet road taken out of use in 1957. The new inlet road can also be seen with the white gate across it.

W. Scaplehorn

English Electric type '3' No. D6926 shunts at Colbren Junction in 1964/65. *W. Scaplehorn*

An unidentified English Electric type '3' shunts at Craig-y-Nos. *W. Scaplehorn*

Class '66' No. 66191 on an Aberthaw train being loaded at Onllwyn washery.   *Author*

Driver Dave Llewellyn (*right*) with shunter Mike Marshall and No. 66191 at Onllwyn washery. In the background the wagon is being loaded by a mechanical shovel. These photographs were taken with the permisssion of Celtic Energy, Onllwyn.   *Author*

Chapter Five

Rough Trips

Under normal conditions, and that was 80 per cent of the time, you would expect to have a reasonable day with a steam engine. There were some locomotives that were excellent steamers and you got to know these and it would make your day if you were allocated one – they were usually engines that had recently returned from Swindon and were in sound running condition. But, sometimes, you would find yourself in very different circumstances with a rogue engine, but not necessarily the locomotive's fault.

One turn I can remember well was relieving Swindon men at Severn Tunnel with a back working. We had worked an Acton coal train from Jersey Marine Jn yard with a '72XX' and had relief at the Tunnel. We had gone into the relief cabin and reported to the inspector and he said that a train of pools had just left Lydney for Port Talbot, so we made a can of tea and sat down for half an hour with the rest of the crews waiting to relieve trains.

After some considerable time the inspector shouted out, 'Depot set, train passing East box' so we collected our belongings and guard and made our way to the station reception roads. When we arrived we could see a '28XX' class pulling into the long reception road behind the platform. My mate remarked this did not look good, you could see that they were having a bad time with the blower full on. The train pulled up to the end of the road and stopped by the water column; we climbed up and the fireman looked dead on his feet and the driver was pretty grimy too. They had tidied up a bit and pulled some coal down, the fireman had made an effort and had washed down the footplate for relief but the clock showed only about 110 lb. and half a glass of water.

The Swindon driver said that they were down to a batch of bad coal and after leaving Gloucester they had struggled to keep going and had advised control that there was a problem. They left and my mate went with them saying, 'Do what you can mate', so I got out the pricker and inspected the fire. I tried to feel the bar but it was a mass of clinker and I realised straight away that we were not going anywhere with this fire, so I put the pricker away and took my overall coat off because I had a considerable amount of work to perform. I put the bag in the tender and turned on the water and left it to run on a slow filling.

I looked out for my mate before starting and he was walking back from the cabin. He said that we had three choices, we could go to Severn Tunnel shed for a few drams of fresh coal or change the engine, but we would have to prepare the new locomotive, or travel to Cardiff where one would be waiting ready prepared. I said that we needed at least half an hour to clean the existing fire and there was no way we could leave the Tunnel without fresh coal. The water was now overflowing so my mate turned the water off and pulled the bag out.

My mate asked if there was any good coal in the tender enough to get us to Canton. I said there could be but we would have to dig for it. The guard now appeared and asked what was happening; we told him that we were going to clean the fire and look for some good coal but this could take about 30 minutes.

The driver asked the guard to contact control and tell them we needed a new engine at Canton. The guard told us the load was 60 pools.

My mate went into the tender to look for good coal and I got stuck into the fire. I got the bar out and tried to find the firebars, with some difficulty I lifted a section under the doors and it came up in a large slab of clinker about three feet square. I broke this up and went to look for the fire shovel and found we did not have one. My mate looked over the top of the tender and said that there was a pannier tank in the yard and to ask him for his. The fireman was on his own and I told him of my problem. There was a short tank engine fire shovel on the back of the bunker he told me to leave it in the 'four foot' and he would pick it up later.

Returning to our engine, my mate told me that he had found some of the bottom coal which looked okay and he was shovelling it forward for me. I went back to work on the fire and lifted out all the section of clinker that I had raised with the pannier fire shovel, dropping this over the side of the steps. I then got the pricker out and pushed all the good loose fire to the front end of the box. I returned the bar into the fire and started to raise all the middle section of clinker and after some difficulty it again came up in a large slab section which I again broke up and I shovelled it out over the side. By this time I was soaking wet with sweat, and sat down for a drink of water. My mate was still looking for good coal but was beginning to complain; it was a good job he was one of the younger drivers, the older men would not have done it and probably left it to the fireman.

After shovelling out all the remaining clinker from the middle and back sections of the firebox, I again got the pricker out and pulled all the burnt live coal from the front of the box to the rear of the box, levelling it out over the bars. I shovelled some of the coal which my mate had brought from the back of the tender and started to build up the fire again. The coal started to burn quite well and it looked as if my mate had found some good coal; I put all the lumps on making sure that all the small stuff remained in the tender.

I was unable to lift any more clinker because there was no more live fire to push over the bars if I removed the clinker from the front end and we only had a small fire shovel anyway. I put the blower on to excite the fire and within no time the fire perked up and looked quite healthy and the steam pressure started to rise. After a bit I put the injector on to put some water in the boiler, which by now had dropped to a ¼ of a glass.

I was already feeling all in and my mate was not looking too good either. The guard appeared again and he said that we had been half an hour and how were we doing? My mate told him we would be about 15 minutes. I turned the injector off, the boiler was now half full. I put a few more shovels on and kept the blower on and the steam was now showing 140 lb., put the injector on again, we needed at least ¾ of a boiler before we took off. Finally the clock showed 160 lb. and I filled the bucket with water so we could have a wash. The guard reappeared and the driver told him to ask for the road. As he walked back to his van, the board dropped 'off' with a clang and we were now in a position to try and get to Cardiff where a new engine awaited.

The injector was on again, the water was in the top nut and steam at 160 lb., not too bad. I turned the blower down and we moved off, tip from the guard, down the relief line to Tunnel West box where we stopped for a main line train to pass. As we waited we had the last of the tea; the pannier tank whose fire shovel I had borrowed was shunting in the yard and when they came near to us I shouted that his shovel was in the four foot at the hump end, the fireman waved and wished us good luck. I had dropped the flap and under normal circumstances the locomotive would have blown off by now but she was simmering, and I decided to get the bar out again and lift the front section of clinker and was reasonably successful. I put the bar away and got the pricker out and pulled some of the clinker back under the door. I put another round of coal over the grate. A passenger train went by, we were signalled across to the main line and we were away. My mate said he couldn't understand why we had not continued down the relief line as usual. As soon as we had gone a short distance I could tell that the engine was not happy, I put the blower on a bit, my mate looked at me saying, 'Fingers crossed, it's flat all the way to Canton'.

We ran reasonably well through Magor but when I put the injector on the steam dropped back; with the boiler at ¾ full I knocked it off and allowed the steam to improve but it did not. I inspected the fire and could see that there was a dull glow in most parts of the box so put another round of coal over the box and increased the blower. I got the pricker out and ran it through the fire, black smoke belching out of the chimney. It did improve a bit, but when I put the injector on the steam dropped back to 140 lb. so I increased the blower again.

We were now approaching East Usk and on to Newport Bridge where we were signalled into the middle through roads and brought to a stand. The steam was still on 140 lb. with the injector still on, we gained ¾ in the glass. I turned the injector off and again put the pricker through the fire with the blower on, the board dropped 'off' and we pulled up the slight grade into the tunnels, taking the left-hand tunnel, blower on now, steam at 140 lb., boiler dropping to ½, out the other side and we were signalled down the relief, passing AD Jn and Ebbw shed on the right. My mate cut the regulator down to its lowest possible opening and we trundled down the relief towards Marshfield, steam around 160 lb., injector on, steam drops back, pricker into the fire again, blower increased, injector off, steam regains a few pounds, injector on again, steam drops back. This is how it was all the way to Pengam, but by then the water was down to half a glass with just 100 lb. on the clock. My mate stopped at Pengam box and told the signalman about our problems and that we had had a rough time and to advise the Canton men that we were coming off at the station. He was a little bemused and we explained that we were having an engine change at the station. We pulled away down the loop limping badly with ¼ glass and 100 lb. steam to Newtown West where we stopped for a 'blow up'; my mate went into the cabin to ring the signalman and ask him for a 15 minute spell to 'blow up' for steam.

I put the pricker in again and pulled the fire through with the blower hard on and the injector was also on. I finally got ½ glass of water showing with 100 lb. on the clock. My mate climbed aboard and said that the Canton men wouldn't go to Port Talbot with the train because the fireman was only a passed cleaner, so we were to leave the train at Penarth Curve and take the engine to shed. The signal was lowered, by this time we had 140 lb. on the gauge. We pulled out from Newtown onto the grade into Cardiff station with the blower full on through the station, ¼ glass of water, 100 lb. on the clock, around the curve and into the reception roads at Penarth South Curve. After taking the engine to shed at Canton, we then had the long walk back to Cardiff station and home 'on the cushions'. 'Glad to see the back of that one mate'; I agreed.

Another rough trip, but for a different reason, which comes to mind was a control turn from Felin Fran. At Swansea Eastern Depot we had a few 'control trains'; they would run as required by control, for traffic requirements; one day you could be running to West Wales and the next to Cardiff or Severn Tunnel.

On this particular day we worked engine and van to Felin Fran and our locomotive was a '52XX'. The '52XX' 2-8-0T at Swansea Eastern Depot at this time were Nos. 5210, 5221, 5232, 5240 and 5246. There were also two '72XX' 2-8-2T, Nos. 7224 and 7226. We left East Dock with our brake van in tow and ran through the burrows on to Jersey Marine Jn where we took the line to Llandarcy and onto the Swansea District line, though Lonlas tunnel down the bank into Felin Fran and down the loop to Felin Fran West siding.

The guard was met by the trainmeeter who told him his train was in No. 4 road. He disappeared into the siding to take his tally and after the trainmeeter had cut off the brake van and put the van hand brake on we pulled forward into the shunting spur and blew three, 'inside the points'. The signalman at the West box reversed the points and the dummy (ground shunting signal) came 'off' for us to join our train in the sidings, the shunter coupled up and we waited for the guard to return. By this time I was building the fire up and making sure that the boiler was full because we had a very heavy climb after leaving the yard straight onto the bank and into Llangyfelach tunnel and on to Llangyfelach box at the top of the bank. The guard eventually appeared and said we had a full load of duff (small coal) for the power station at Pembrey; the trainmeeter phoned the bobby in the box and said that we were ready to leave.

'72XX' class 2-8-2T No. 7207 of Landore shed passes through Neath (General) station.
Robert Thomas

The board dropped 'off' for the main line and we started to pull out of the yard onto the District Line. At once the driver, Joffer Reed, said that this was a heavy train. We struggled out of the yard and cleared the siding points and dropped back on to the brake van in the loop. The guard coupled up and he climbed up into his van took the hand brake off and gave us the 'right away' one hand above the head with a little wave.

We struggled to get away from Felin Fran making a very slow pace. The driver said, 'This is an extremely heavy load and I would say that we have been overloaded by the guard'. By this time we were crossing over the main road river bridge and using full regulator into the bank. I was building the fire up at the back and keeping the front end low, the injector was on and would stay on, with the huge blast the fire was extremely hot and the engine was 'blowing off'. The second injector went on, as I worked hard keeping the back end full and the front end low. The driver was now looking troubled saying we were definitely over our load for the bank.

Our train was barely moving and we were going so slowly you could jump off and jump back on quite easily; to make matters worse we were chimney first so that when we hit the tunnel the sulphur would come back into the cab. By this time we were in the cutting and nearing the tunnel mouth. The driver said, 'Do we stop and get assistance or go for it?' We decided to go for it and as we entered the tunnel a down train flew past filling the bore with smoke making our task even more difficult. We were now into the tunnel and still going very slowly, although the engine was steaming well; the boiler was full and 'blowing off'. We were now well into the tunnel and the blast of the engine was rebounding from the tunnel roof on to the engine and into our cab, the sulphur starting to fill our mouths. The driver said, 'Wet your handkerchief and put it around your nose and mouth', he did the same. I examined the fire and attended to its requirements, filled up the back end and closed the flap and left it.

The sulphur was now getting to us, and my mate told me to climb down the outside steps and get as low as I could; he did the same on his side of the engine. He said, 'Forget about the fire, if we stop, we stop'. We both clung to the cabside steps where the air was not so bad and waited for the end of the tunnel.

We eventually came out into the fresh air, and we immediately climbed back onto the footplate to attend to our tasks. The locomotive had turned white from the effects of the sulphur; inside the cab it was not so bad but outside it was as if a frost had covered the engine.

The fire now needed coal, the front end was low and was drawing air through the firegrate and making a humming noise. Steam pressure was down to 150 lb. and I had to get the pricker out to push fire from the back to the front to stop further deterioration of the fire. The humming stopped and the pressure held at 160 lb. I built up the back end again and we seemed to have overcome the immediate problem. We had by now cleared the cutting and were nearing the box at the top of the bank also the approach to Velindre Steel sidings on the right-hand side.

The signalman was in the window of the box and was concerned because we had taken so long in this section. The driver had come over to my side and shouted to the bobby that he thought we had been overloaded. The signalman asked if we wanted to go in at Pontlliw loop but the driver said 'No, we'll run

One of the large BR-built 0-6-0PTs of '94XX' class, No. 9448, is employed to assist an unidentified 'Hall' class up the bank out of Neath *en route* to Swansea. The Neath yard west end pilot was used to bank trains up Skewen bank. *Norman Jones*

Heavy snowfall provided challenging conditions for railwaymen. In this view a pair of pannier tanks, with snow ploughs fitted, are seen on the isolated Colbren to Penwyllt section on the Neath & Brecon line. *W. Scaplehorn*

them down the bank' and waved. We ran down the bank through Pontlliw and Grovesend, over the viaduct at Morlais Jn, through Llangennech and Bynea stations, and into Llandilo Jn yards, through Llanelli station, and on to Old Castle, eventually slowing for the approach roads for Pembrey Power station and into the yard there.

We waited the guard's appearance with interest and when he did appear he looked very guilty saying he was very sorry. The driver laid into him saying he had put him and the fireman through a hell of a trip through the tunnel and the signalman at Llangyfelach was obviously concerned, because he thought we had failed in the tunnel. He most likely had reported this to control, so expect some sort of backlash from above, the driver said. 'Just out of curiosity, how much were we overloaded?' The guard said equivalent to 10 class one's: that equates to about eight extra wagons.

We then sat down and put the can on the fire and had a cup of tea and ate our sandwiches saying we were very lucky to have come out of the incident without too much trouble. If we had failed in the tunnel it would have caused a considerable problems. Another day in the life of a loco crew. The return working on this duty was taking empty wagons (pools) from Pembrey to Jersey Marine Jn yard for storage until required.

The final rough trip to be described was caused by adverse weather. When working an afternoon report duty, the fireman for the 5 pm to Graig Merthyr (Swansea District line) did not turn up; I was given the job.

On this duty the engine worked off shed, always a '94XX' large pannier tank. I will always remember the day in question because it was snowing very heavily and drifting. We left shed at Swansea East Dock after preparing the engine and taking water at the shed water column which had its brazier lit to stop the column freezing up. It was getting dark and we progressed to the shed dummy signal, this was covered with snow which I cleaned off. I went down to the phone and rang the bobby to ask for the road; climbing back on the footplate, the signal came off with a clang and shifted the rest of the snow that covered it. We proceeded to the brake van road quietly because it was now so bad that we could only see 50 yards or so. We stopped by the East Dock box to take instructions from the signalman who told us that if we had to turn any hand points to check to see if the blades were closed because of the packing snow, but the road was set okay. We joined the brake van in the siding covered with snow and coupled up; the guard arrived and told the driver that we had to pick up empties in the Violet Sidings in King's Dock for Graig Merthyr Colliery.

The snow was now ankle deep and getting worse and the wind was blowing quite fiercely. This type of engine was crew-friendly but the snow was still getting into the cab through the open cab door area but melted on contact with warm metal. Again passing the box, only now visible by the glow from its internal lights, we progressed to the signal which we could see with difficulty. We ran through to Prince of Wales Dock Junction, passing the box on the right, but slowing down at every signal to look up at the position of the arm. We arrived at Burrows box with its home signal 'on', again only picking this up an engine's length from the signal.

We waited for some time, but no movement: the driver said, 'Mate you will have to walk to the box and tell the bobby we have arrived'. This was a requirement of Rule 55. The snow was now very deep in places. I said to my mate, 'If I don't get back, tell my girlfriend I love her'. We laughed as he said something that is not printable. I found it very difficult to walk but eventually got to the box and confronted the signalman who said: 'Good grief, a live snowman, keep out, I'll sign the book'. He advised me that the points were frozen in the Violet Sidings and control was looking for other empties for us. With that the phone rang and control told the signalman that there were empties at Jersey Marine, so the signalman lowered the signal for my mate and he pulled down opposite the box for me.

It was now snowing very heavily so we ran slowly stopping at every board to see if it was clear, eventually arriving at Jersey Marine and stopped outside the yard on the main line. The guard climbed down from his van and was immediately up to his knees in snow; he made his way to the shunter's cabin in the yard but we lost sight of him just 10 yards from the locomotive.

The signal was lowered and we ran to the signal box and waited for the points, after a couple of trys to turn them the signalman was eventually successful. We ran into the yard and put the brake van onto the yard pilot and coupled up to the empties in the yard. The guard remarked that he couldn't see us getting far tonight; after walking around the train he returned and told the driver that we had 40 empties on. The pilot attached the brake van then we waited for some time before the signal was lowered and we left the yard slowly.

Very slowly we proceeded from Jersey Marine around the corner and headed for Jersey North Jn box. We started to climb from Jersey South and the driver began to work the engine. I started firing in earnest; approaching Jersey North we almost stop the train in order to pick out the home signal and find that it is 'off'. The signalman waved from his open window as we pass and we were now out on the Swansea District line and working towards Llandarcy. There are high cuttings here and the snow was beginning to drift into the cutting, we are now working through some deep snow, with snow in some places up to the footplate, but very soft and soon displaced. we again have difficulty seeing the Llandarcy home signal but pick it up as we cut our speed. The signalman was at his open window and shouted across that we had got the road to Felin Fran.

We could now open up and start working the train on this steep grade, we ran into the tunnel at Lonlas not looking for the signal as we are moving too fast to pick it up anyway. The train went over the top of the bank at this point and on a falling gradient through the tunnel. At the other end we hit a snowdrift and it showered the locomotive with snow, but being quite soft snow at this point it gave way to us. We looked at each other but said nothing. Running down the bank into Felin Fran, again we slow down for the signal and find that it is 'off', we look to pick up the next signal slowing down again until we are almost on it; it is 'off'. The driver opened up for the climb to Llangyfelach tunnel; again we run into drifting snow in the cutting before the tunnel but blast into the hole flat out as it is quite steep at this point.

We pound through the tunnel with the engine blowing off and at the other end again hit drifting snow. This blew up all over the locomotive and slowed us down because we did not have the weight of the train behind us. At the top of the bank we slowed down for the signal box; the signalman had his window open and was waving a red light. We stopped and he told us that Graig Merthyr Colliery's locomotive had derailed on frozen points and that we were to work through to Pontardulais with the empties. We had 'got the road' (all sections clear) to Morlais Jn; we waved and started our train, but slip very badly. The train was still on the rising gradient: I pulled the sand levers and after some difficulty we finally got away. Into the short tunnel at Penllergaer and down the bank passing Pontlliw box, the train was throwing up clouds of snow and the weather was not improving at all. We passed Graig Merthyr Colliery transfer siding at Grovesend and ran into Morlais Jn. Slowing down here almost to a stop, we found the signal was 'off' and we ran towards Hendy Jn into the low tunnel into Pontardulais station, but again very slowly, picking up the signal just yards from its position.

The trainmeeter came out onto the platform and told us to pull up clear of the points where the pilot would take our empties off. Moving slowly up through the platform road, we finally heard the pilot blowing three whistles and we stop. I jumped down knee-deep in snow, took the locomotive coupling off and climbed back up onto the footpalte. The pilot eventually moved off with our train and we followed on behind and stopped at the signal to await instructions. We noticed at Pontardulais that there were extra men clearing out snow from points.

The guard eventually joined us and said that he had been talking to the trainmeeter who said that it was complete chaos everywhere, trains had been stopped and snow was building up very badly. The yard foreman then came over and asked the driver if he knew the road to Swansea Victoria, which he did. I said, 'I don't'; he replied, 'You don't count'. The foreman said that there was perishable traffic here and the train that usually picked it up was stuck in Llandovery. The signal was lowered and we ran into the yard and took water, again the column brazier was burning well. Moving onto the train, the shunter coupled up and the guard told us that we had 12 vanfits on for Victoria goods and then home, engine and van. 'Put the can on mate, let's have a cup of tea.' I got the can boiling iron out and within seconds the can water boiled on the fire and we are all drinking tea and having a sandwich.

The foreman came over and said that when we were ready, we were to back onto the brake van and we would have the road to Gowerton. We finished our tea, the guard got down into the snow, we backed the train onto the van and waited for the signal. This shunting movement was only achieved with the shunter walking back to the engine every time because when the shunter moved away five yards he could not be seen. The signal dropped 'off' with a clang, and we moved into former LMS terrritory where I had never been before. Ariving at Gowerton, the branch passenger was waiting for us with a former LMS tank engine in charge. 'Probably the last local from Victoria', my mate said. We stopped by the signal and waited events, the branch passenger moved off and we waited and waited. The signal eventually came 'off'; these signals were upper quadrant as my mate pointed out; he thought they were better signals than our lower quadrant ones. We ran very slowly through Dunvant and then

Killay, not able to see much with the weather so bad, into Mumbles Road and then along Swansea Bay passing the loco shed at Paxton Street with all its lights which we could pick out through the snow and into Victoria station.

The station yard pilot took the vans off us and we pulled up to the board and waited, we made another can of tea and had a sandwich; the pilot reattached our brake van to our locomotive. We were told when the signal came 'off' to run clear of the high level points and work into South Dock high level and contact the shunter. The signal was cleared and we finally climbed into the high level sidings. The shunter here walked over and asked if he could run a short train to High Street. He said that the vans should have worked up to High Street yesterday, the goods department had been shouting for them. He went on to say that most of his yard points were frozen and he was waiting for help to come.

My mate agreed: we picked up the vans, stuck a tail lamp on the hook of the last van and away, dropping them off at the Maliphant sidings at High Street. Finally it was home to Swansea East Depot, firstly running to Wind Street Jn; at Wind Street the signalman could not turn the points for us and I had to get down and clear the snow from them with the fireman's shovel and brush. We then ran past Weavers flour mill and into St Thomas and then, after putting our van away, ran to the shed. What a night, one of the worst I can remember. Next day we found out that 50 per cent of trains booked out of East Dock did not run and we were the last train locomotive to leave shed.

Next day it had stopped snowing and things were returning to some normality. After booking on my mate and I had to relieve the morning snow clearing gang which had been working in Swansea Docks. They came into East Dock sidings with a pannier tank and two brake vans and a gang of permanent way men. We changed guards, the afternoon fitter relieved the morning fitter on the steam lance which was fitted to the front of the locomotive and which was normally used for cleaning engine tubes. This was being used to steam snow from frozen points etc. We were told to work to High Street and clear the snow from the station turntable, it was a bitterly cold day and copious amounts of tea were drunk on this job by all concerned. On the funny side, one of the work gang disappeared into a snow-filled loco pit and had to be rescued. In circumstances of heavy snow the signalman has on call his designated pointsman to help clear or clamp points if necessary. The main problem with points freezing is not so much the points but the point locking slide bars, and if they are not working the signal will not come 'off', so the pointsman has to clamp the points and show a yellow flag to authorize the driver to proceed with caution. But if the pointsman does not turn up for duty the fireman had to do it himself if he wanted to get home.

Chapter Six

Tales of the Trains

Steam to Severn Tunnel Junction

Working a '72XX' class 2-8-2T to Severn Tunnel in the late 1950s was an overtime job; working slow goods trains between South Wales and Severn Tunnel was a very slow process, because we had to give way to all other trains due to our lowly headcode. We were put into every loop possible and at the long loops at Tremains and Miskin you would possibly be in behind two other trains, and it was common practice for the signalman to stick up two fingers to you when passing the box at Tremains or Miskin, to indicate two trains already in the loop.

When you booked on at Swansea Eastern Depot you would read your notices, and get your engine number from the booking-on office and proceed to your engine, usually a '72XX' class or '42XX' 2-8-0T on the London coal trains. On this occasion, it was No. 7224. You checked your locomotive, which had been prepared by the shed prep crew; boiler ¾ full, fire in good condition but needed building up, steam possibly 160 lb. on the gauge. The driver comes aboard, asks if everything is okay, checks his lubricator for oil bubbles in the glasses and tells me to take the handbrake off. We plod to the outward spur of the shed and the fireman drops down from the engine to phone the signalman at the Eastern Depot box asking for the road. Eventually the dummy drops off and we progress through the goods yard passing the signal box to pick up the brake van in the mileage yard.

The guard takes particulars of the engine number, driver's name and tells us we are to proceed engine and van to Jersey Marine Jn to pick up our coal train. We leave East Dock passing the Burrows with Danygraig engine shed in the background with all its dock tanks outside the shed, pass Jersey Marine station and into Jersey Marine yards. We would then propel the brakevan into the yard and the yard pilot would take it and run it though the yard and put it on the back of our train. We backed onto our train and waited for the guard to take the tally and examine the train; he would eventually arrive to say we were six over the load for Stormy and would need the banker. The train was all London coal for Acton yard. Once the guard told the trainmeeter everything was all right he would go into his cabin and ring the signalman for the road. The signal would be lowered and we would pull out of the yard, the fireman looking for the guard's tip that he was in his brakevan, with this with done he would start firing, building his fire up for Stormy bank.

The '42' and '72' class engines were happy with a big fire unlike the panniers. The fireman would build up the back end of the box and keep the front end low, this type of fire worked well on these big engines. Tractive effort on the '72XX' was 33,170 lb., they had 2,500 gallon tanks and were over 44 ft long, carrying 6 tons of coal; total weight with coal and water was 92½ tons.

We were by this time on the District Line and passing the rear of Neath shed, then through Court Sart and passing the back of Briton Ferry station. Here we

Mogul No. 6361 carries a 'B' headcode as it works a down stopping train into Briton Ferry.
Norman Jones

'42XX' class 2-8-0T No. 5222 of Ebbw Junction shed works through Neath with a coal train bound for London which it will work as far as Severn Tunnel Jn.   *Robert Thomas*

'28XX' class 2-8-0 No. 2867 runs main line at Briton Ferry with a van train bound for Banbury, picking up at Court Sart east end. *Norman Jones*

Pannier tank No. 3617 is employed on banking duties at Neath and is seen assisting an unidentified 'Castle' class with a Swansea-bound train. Trials with bankers employed as asssitant engines in front of, and behind, the train engine were unsuccessful. Finally the banker ran, uncoupled, at the rear of the train. *Norman Jones*

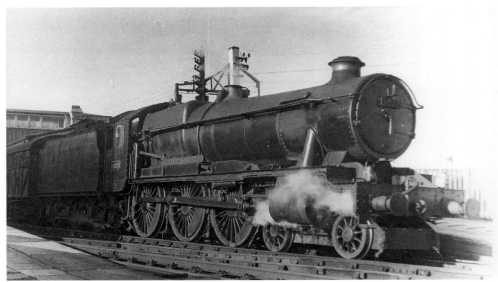

The last 4-6-0 'County' class locomotive to remain in service was No. 1029 *County of Worcester*. She is seen here at Neath.   *Norman Jones*

Prairie tank No. 5573 takes (too much) water at Neath after working in over the Vale of Neath line.   *Norman Jones*

were brought to a stand to wait for a main line train to go through. I would drop the firehole flap and put the injector on to keep the engine from blowing off, put a few shovels behind the doors (back end of firebox) and wait. After the London passenger has passed at speed, the signal drops 'off', the fireman looks for the tip from the guard and away onto the main line passing the Briton Ferry yards, on to Baglan Moors and into Port Talbot station, through Port Talbot yards and we then take the loop signal for Margam West and cut down our speed to gain the loop line. From here we would plod quietly on the up relief line to Margam Moors for the banker, which was waiting at the top end of the yard. We blew our whistle, the crew came out of the cabin and climbed up onto '42XX' 2-8-0T No. 5216 and ran down the yard onto the rear of our train.

The trainmeeter then phoned the box so we could progress, but no luck, an up train was due. After a time an up fast vacuum-fitted goods flew through, still no luck, another vacuum goods went through, then the board dropped and we were away, the front engine giving two crows on the whistle. The banker answered with two crows, and out onto the main line for the long climb up Stormy bank. By this time the flap was down and I was examining the fire with my shovel putting a few shovels of coal where needed. The blower was put on a little to excite the fire after our long stay at the Moors, steam pressure was down to 180 lb. and the fire was not yet warmed up. The driver was now onto the bank and using full regulator, causing the fire to jump about. I loosened up the fire with the pricker, pushing hot coals to the front, pricker out, a few shovels behind the doors, this made a big difference and the clock moved to 185 lb. More coal was needed; six shovels to front end, close flap, short spell, drop flap, six shovels to rear of box, examine front end and close flap. The water was by now down to ¾ of a glass, so the small injector was put on and left on. The fire was now getting hot, but steam pressure drops to 180 lb. when the second injector goes on; drop flap, the fire is now very hot burning my face, another six shovels front end and a few around back end, close flap, pressure now holding at 185 lb. Looking back I can see the banker is working flat out; by this time we were coming up to Pyle West box, a real crescendo of steam power blasting out and a very impressive sight. I am still firing, keeping the back end full and front end low, all of a sudden the engine blows off and I look at the clock: 200 lb. red mark achieved.

The driver looks at me, smiling; sweat is dripping off my face and I am down to my tee shirt with my overall coat put to one side. By now we are passing Pyle station signal box, the signalman is watching us through an open window. Again looking back I can see the banker blowing off; another round of firing, six front end, keeping back end built up, by this time coal is up to the firehole door and lapping the rim of the doors. The second injector is on and knocks the clock back to 190 lb. After checking the boiler water level with the blow down lever, I shut down the second injector, steam regains pressure and blows off at 200 lb. Driver says, 'Good engine this, steaming well'; we were now coming up to Stormy summit and we could not yet see the Stormy home signal due to the road bridge but as soon as we had passed this we could see the loop board was 'off'. I said, 'In the loop, mate', he acknowledged and I immediately dropped the flap as the engine was blowing off. Our steam pressure dropped to 180 lb.

'42XX' class 2-8-0T No. 5225 on a down steel coil train at Court Sart. *Norman Jones*

'42XX' class 2-8-0T No. 5239 shows an 'H' headcode as it stands ready to pull out of Briton Ferry yard. The fireman looks back from the cab for the guard's signal. *Norman Jones*

'Off the road'. Pannier tank No. 3621 was on a ballast train through Neath station when one of the 'Grampus' wagons became derailed with the author one of those looking on.

(Both) Norman Jones

An early view along the platform at Neath. *Lens of Sutton Collection*

A view along the platform at Neath looking towards Briton Ferry in the 1950s. The middle road and crossovers were taken out in 1967. *Norman Jones*

but we were now over the worst of it and had taken the loop points and the driver was already easing the regulator.

Once the banker blew three whistles 'inside clear', the signalman would reverse the points and the main line signals would be lowered. By this time we would have come into line with the water column, I would jump up onto the tank and put the bag in, the driver would then operate the water release handle and we would top up our tanks. A Paddington-bound passenger passed working hard and blowing his whistle; we must have checked him on Stormy, probably caught a distant 'on' at Pyle East, and he was saying so. The tanks are now full, and the banker has gone back to Margam; we return to the footplate, and after checking the fire, I was just about to climb onto the bunker to level the coal when the board drops 'off', so back onto the footplate, the driver opens up and moves us out onto the main line and away down the bank into Bridgend. At Tremains, as we pass the box the bobby holds up two fingers, meaning in the loop behind two, but as we reach the first goods train he moves off and drops down to the loop exit signal and puts the bag in at the water column.

We know we will have about 30 minutes here at least so the can goes on, sandwiches come out and we have a break. The fire cools down, boiler ¾ full, leaving room to keep it quiet, pressure at 200 lb. blowing off quietly. A passenger train passes on the main line, the front train gets the road, we follow, dropping down to water column to top up our tanks. The water column at this point was next to the main road and you could look down at passing cars. Checking the fire, the front end is low so six shovels front end, a few around back end; another train passes on the main line, the loop board drops 'off' and we move out onto the main line. When passing the box the signalman shouts that we have got the road for the bank, knowing this the driver can 'run the train' into the bank. He waves in response and looks at me; the fire looks a bit thick, putting the pricker in, loosens it up a bit, coal drops at the front end and I immediately realise that I have to build this up. I place six shovels of coal at the front end, a few behind the doors, the driver is now moving the train hard but keeping full regulator for Pencoed. Approaching Pencoed Crossing box and driver now puts the regulator to full as the train bites into the bank, steam pressure is holding at 180 lb. the water is down to ¾ glass. I put the small injector on and leave it on, drop the flap, and place six shovels down front, close the flap, short break, six in back end, short spell, finally six shovels front end. This would continue until we reached Llanharan platform, by this time we were at Bryn Y Gwian crossing and full into the climb with the engine blowing off. This bank was not as steep as Stormy and did not require a banker.

We had now reached the station at Llanharan with the CWS Milk depot to the right, reaching the top of the bank passing Llanharan West box, I drop the flap, put the injector on, and steam drops back to 180 lb. We straddle the top of the bank and then descend the long down grade into Llantrisant, over the level crossing and through the platforms, with the Cowbridge bay to our right. We are put into the long loop at Miskin and finally come up to the train we were behind in Tremains loop. Looking at the fire a few blue flames are showing and realise that some parts of the firebox are beginning to clinker up, I report this to the driver and get the bar out to push it through the bars to clear any clinker

'Hall' class 4-6-0 No. 6932 *Burwarton Hall* of Cardiff (Canton) shed leaves Neath on an up express.   *Norman Jones*

'Hall' class 4-6-0 No. 4982 *Acton Hall* stands at Neath on a down stopping train.   *Norman Jones*

BR Standard 'Britannia' pacific No. 70007 *Coeur-de-Lion* climbs Skewen bank with a down express in 1963.   *Norman Jones*

Swindon-built BR Standard class '2MT' 2-6-2T No. 82000 of Treherbert shed takes water at the end of Neath platform before returning to Treherbert.   *Robert Thomas*

'Manor' class 4-6-0 No. 7826 *Longworth Manor* works a vacuum-fitted goods train through Neath. The engine was shedded at Carmarthen.   *Norman Jones*

Neyland-allocated '2251' class 0-6-0 No. 2226 has arrived at Neath with a stopping train. Notice the ROD tender.   *Norman Jones*

that has formed, after doing this I can get an indication of the condition of the fire. The bar went through without too much trouble and I so inform the driver.

We had now broken the back of the trip with no more banks to contend with; after putting the bar away which was glowing red hot, I had to rebuild the fire and I put about six shovels around the back ends. By this time we had dropped down to the water column at the end of the loop, and after topping up the tanks, the driver went round with his oil can topping up where necessary. I now have time to trim the bunker, after a while the board drops 'off' and we are away, passing St George's Crossing box and on to Peterston, into the dip, guard puts his brake on through the dip to keep the couplings tight. At Leckwith Jn the loop board is 'off', and we run down the loop to Canton, stopping opposite the signal box and shed. The signalman shouts over, 'Control wants to speak to the driver'. My driver says, 'Here we go, no relief'. Speaking to control on the phone, he comes to the signal box window and shouts over: 'Do you fancy a trip to Severn Tunnel?' I reply with thumbs up, so far it has taken us approximately six hours to get this far. Control also tells us the engine is working to Swindon.

The guard by this time had come down and the driver breaks the news, saying if he did not want to go on to the Tunnel, there was a guard at the station to relieve him. He decides to stay and walks back but we are brought to a stand in Cardiff centre road, with a London passenger about to leave. We follow this down the bank into Newtown West through to Newtown East and Pengam yards; by this time we are on the goods avoiding line and are running well. We get held up at Marshfield for a short time but eventually get to Ebbw Jn with the AD Yards to our right, into Gaer tunnel and into Newport centre road, here the signal is 'on' and we wait for a passenger train to clear.

Since leaving Cardiff the road has been fairly flat and the firehole flap was down most of the time to stop the engine blowing off and was quite happy at 180 lb. We again get the road and continue up the relief line, through the Newport East yards, past Llanwern Steel Works, through Magor, over the flyover at Bishton to gain the left-hand side for the approach to Tunnel yards, through Undy and into the big expanse of Severn Tunnel Jn. Passing the West box the loop signal is lowered, and I again need to get the bar out and loosen any clinker for my relief. A few more shovels under the doors, up onto the bunker, and trim the coal, finally out with the pep pipe to wash down the footplate. By this time we were rolling into Severn Tunnel East yards and stopped behind the Middle box, waiting for relief.

We put all our items together, our food boxes into our bags, and our coats on, leaving the flap down with steam on 180 lb., the boiler ¾ full. Severn Tunnel men jump up, the fireman asking if I had put the bar through which I confirm. We walk over to the relief cabin, report to the inspector, who asked if we want to work back. We tell him we don't want to, he smiles and tells us to make our way home 'on the cushions'. That was that, we were now on nine hours and had to get back to our depot. We would probably be able to book off within our 12 hours to catch our turn for the next day, otherwise we would have to come on 'after rest' and lose our next booked turn.

'56XX' class 0-6-2T No. 5649 of Aberdare runs through Neath & Brecon Junction with a mixed freight for Swansea docks.   *Robert Thomas*

'Grange' class 4-6-0 No. 6819 *Highnam Grange* of Pontypool Road has just arrived at Neath in this 1964 view.   *Robert Thomas*

Ex-LMS Stanier '8F' class 2-8-0 No. 48438 of Llanelly shed crosses into Neath yard with a mixed freight in 1963. *Robert Thomas*

'16XX' class 0-6-0PT No. 1645 is on duty as the Neath East beat pilot engine in the summer of 1959. It is seen standing outside the Ministry of Supply factory. *R. Grant*

'Castle' class 4-6-0 No. 5038 *Morlais Castle* of Old Oak Common passes through Neath station on a down parcels train.   *Norman Jones*

'Castle' class 4-6-0 No. 5072 *Hurricane* of Landore runs light engine into Swansea (High Street).
                                                                              Hugh Daniels

The Llandarcy Tanks

We were having a cup of tea at Cardiff platform relief cabin and we are under instruction to relieve the down Gloucester-Llandarcy tank train. We had advised the signalman at the main box that we were in the relief cabin; eventually the phone rang and the signalman said that the train was passing Pengam and should be in the station within 10 minutes, but that there was a problem with the engine. Food away, wash up and walk onto the platform and wait, we found an empty seat and sat down. My mate said that if there was a problem with the engine it may have to come off. Eventually the train pulled into the station with steam blowing quite badly from the front end of a 'Hall' class locomotive. It came to rest in the centre roads opposite us, we walked across to the engine and climbed aboard. The Gloucester driver said that he contacted the signalman at Pengam for an engine change as when they were passing Marshfield the piston gland packing had blown. This did not have any effect on the capabilities of the locomotive but the steam was obscuring the driver's view and the noise was quite startling. The Gloucester men climbed down and left us to it.

I looked around the firebox and found quite a large box of fire with three-quarters of water in the glass, the footplate washed down and coal had been pulled down in the tender. The driver decided to walk back to the cabin and phone control and advise them of the problem.

The control advised the driver that arrangements had been made for the engine to go to shed at Canton where a fresh engine was waiting for us. My mate climbed back up into the cab and advised me of this; with that the guard appeared and asked what was happening. We told him that we had to change locomotives and did not know how long we would be. He was a Severn Tunnel guard who was only working to Port Talbot.

After uncoupling the engine I walked to the phone to contact the signalman and said that we were ready to change engines at Canton. As I was walking back the signal went to green. We dropped down the slight incline into Canton and put our defective engine on the coal stage with a large fire; the fire dropper would not be too happy with that. My mate went to look for the shed staff and told them about the problem, he came back and said that they knew about it.

We went into the shed office and they told us that our engine was one of Landore's 'Castles' in the front of the shed. It was going back after repairs.

We made our way to the shed yard and there we found our 'Castle' No. 5014 *Goodrich Castle* with the shed staff on the footplate. The fire was low and the steam pressure was only 120 lb. but everything else was satisfactory. The shed driver told my mate that he had oiled up and was ready to go and the water tank was okay.

They climbed down and were gone; my driver had a look at the fire and told me to start building up the back end, by the time we left the station it should be all right. We moved up to the shed signal and I went down to the phone to tell the signalman who we were. The down Swansea went by and as we waited another fast goods train passed and we eventually got the road. We pulled out of the yard, steam now up to 160 lb. and up the slight incline to the station and

'Castle' class No. 4097 *Kenilworth Castle* leaves Neath with a down parcels train. The postman waits to cross the barrow crossing with mail. *Norman Jones*

'Castle' class 7019 *Fowey Castle* of Bristol (Bath Road) works a Swansea-Bristol express through Neath as an engine crew look on. *Norman Jones*

into the middle roads. I jumped down and coupled up, put the vacuum bags together, took the lamp off the tender and asked my mate what code we were. He replied, 'Left and middle, through freight'. By this time the guard had appeared and he said, 'Posh aren't we?' looking at the 'Castle'. My mate was down on the ground and we all looked around the locomotive *Goodrich Castle*. My mate said, 'I don't think this is a Landore loco', and we walked around to the front and looked at the shed plate, 81A. 'It's an Old Oak engine, I hope they know what they are doing'.

I looked at the fire which I had been building up nicely, water in the top nut, steam at 200 lb. I looked back to see the guard climbing into his van, the signal changes to green; 'It's down the goods loop, mate', we pull away, tip from the guard, driver blows the whistle and away. I now look again at the fire, this grate is big: 30 square ft compared to our normal '42XX' which is 20 square ft. In the past I had only worked light engine trips with these engines from the depot to Landore and never on a train. My driver said: 'These are good steamers, the fire they like is large back end and low front end, so make it look easy mate'. There was plenty of room on the footplate on a 'Castle' and you had to position yourself midway between the tender and the fire hole door and start shovelling. I was building up the back end and putting a few down the front, we were by this time at Leckwith Jn and had come to a stop, with the loop board 'on', main line board 'off'; they were semaphore signals here, Cardiff was all electric.

After a passenger passed the loop signal came 'off' and away we went. We are now on an up grade and hear the lovely bark of the 'Castle' as we find the weight of the 46 tanks. Out onto the main line passing Leckwith box, a wave to the bobby, by this time we are blowing off but the pressure soon drops back when my mate opens up. I put up the firehold flap and pick the damper up a notch, we are now passing Ely station and signal box, over Ely river bridge, through St Fagan's crossing and under the Wenvoe line bridge. I drop the flap and start shovelling, heavy at the back end, a few around the sides and the front, flap up, the engine blows off, the injector goes on for the first time, with water down to half a glass. Steam is holding at 200 lb. with the injector still on going towards St George's Crossing and Miskin, climbing slightly past Miskin, through Llantrisant platforms, passing the crossing box; here the driver opens up for the bank, the engine sounding lovely. I again look at the fire, it's looking a bit low at the front end, so I put shovels of coal in the light areas of the grate, where the fire has burned low; 10 shovels around the back end, black smoke comes from the chimney, the water drops to ¾ of a glass. I put the injector on, my mate says, 'You should have had a full glass for the pull to Llanharan'. Realising my mistake I cross my fingers and say 'It's a "Castle", it's okay'.

We are now deep into the bank and a near full regulator, steam pressure is holding at 200 lb. with the injector on, I check the fire, the front end is again low. I place a few where it needs it down the front and again put about nine shovels at the rear end, up with the flap. Check the water and it's still at ¾ full with the injector on, and steam pressure is holding at 180 lb. I examine the fire and work a few shovels down the front of the box, the back end is all right; we are now approaching Llanharan but still on the bank. The engine is moving nicely, with a lovely bark from the chimney, steam is holding at 180 lb. with the injector still on and the regulator fully open. Coming to the top of the bank I check the fire, putting a few shovels at the front end, about 10 shovels around the back end and down the sides. We are now over the top and I have dropped the flap, water is down to half a glass; checking the fire again, firing heavily at the front end to keep her quiet and topping the back end up. Through Llanharan platforms we are on the down grade now, the injector is still on and steam pressure is at 220 lb. with a feather of steam from the safety valve. My mate looks at me and smiles, 'Not bad for your first time on a "Castle"'.

The train is now moving well but not for long, we get a distant 'on' and a loop board at Tremains and my mate slows the train. Passing Tremains East, the signalman shouts to tell us we are going in the loop for a passenger to pass.

I black out the front end of the fire to keep the engine quiet, and a few shovels around the back end, leaving the flap down. We drop down through the back of Tremains platforms and down to the signal; we usually put water in here on a '42XX' class but with the 4,000 gallon tender my mate planned to take water at Port Talbot when we changed guards. As soon as we stop a stopping passenger train goes past; he disappears around the corner, and into Bridgend station.

The board comes 'off' and we find the main line, we pass the box on the left and creep slowly towards the station. The fire is looking okay with 220 lb. on the clock; I put the injector on to fill the boiler for the big push 'Stormy Down'. My mate looks across and smiles, 'You're learning' he says. Approaching the station, the signal is at danger as the passenger has still not cleared; as we approach the stop signal drops 'off' but the lower arm distant stays 'on'. We plod slowly into Bridgend station, people are still on the platform with their bags, porters with trolleys are sorting out parcels. The signal at the end of the platform is still 'on'. I feed the front end of the fire and a few shovels around the back end.

With the boiler full I turn the injector off and drop the flap as we come to a stand at the end of the platform. I again inspect the fire and put a few shovels around the back end. We are now ready for the bank, the signal is lowered and we pull away from Bridgend station. We were hoping for a run through Bridgend to help with the bank but it's from a standing start, so my mate tells me to hang on. He opens up to half regulator and runs past the goods yards really going for the bank. The blast from the 'Castle' is music to the ears, as we dig into Stormy bank, the engine is now ¾ regulator and picking up speed. We pound into the bank, full regulator now passing the farm bridge and two-thirds into the climb; water drops to ¾ of a glass with the injector on, steam pressure is down to 200 lb. We pound up Stormy but we are slowing due to the steep grade.

After a round of firing the clock stands at 180 lb. pressure with the injector still on. I get the pricker out and run it through the fire with the doors partially closed to keep the heat off my body. I again start firing, back end, a few around the low areas in the front, not too many though as the pricker has done the trick, steam pressure is now up to 200 lb.

We are now nearing the top of the climb and the steam pressure is holding at 200 lb. with the injector on, the tender water level is down to under half. I am now walking a bit for coal, and the tender needs trimming. We find the top of the bank with steam pressure at 180 lb. We crest the top, passing the box on the right with a wave to the bobby. We run down the bank through Pyle station, with the Porthcawl train waiting in the bay platform and run at speed under the road bridge and into the cutting past Pyle West box and down the bank passing Margam yards and through Margam Halt with all the main line boards 'off'. We get a check at Margam Middle and the loop signal at Margam West, up the slight incline into Port Talbot yards. Passing under the railway bridge that takes the line to Dyffryn Yard we then take the loop line to run down towards the relief cabins near the signal box and crossing, where we come to a stand.

After filling the tender, we regain the footplate and await the shunter. He eventually appears with our new guard who we know as he is from Swansea Eastern Depot. The guard says that there are four tanks in the next road for Llandarcy to pick up; he says that he will cut off behind the vacuum section and we can pull forward to set back into the yard.

We have about 20 tanks as a vacuum head and have to pull out onto the main line to shunt this amount. After picking up the extra tanks we now await the signal for the main line, but a passenger train passes and stops at Port Talbot platform. When he clears we leave the yard, we now have 50 tanks on for Llandarcy.

I check my fire, a few down the front, the back end looks all right. I am beginning to work my fire down now, it's nearing the end of our shift, about an hour to go. We are now working through Baglan Moors into Briton Ferry yards and through the station onto the District Line past the rear of Neath loco shed and onto the start of the climb to Llandarcy. I put the pricker into the fire and push some of the burnt coals through to the front, I put about 10 shovels around the back end and put the flap up, steam pressure is 200 lb., the boiler looks good with water at the top of the glass. Over the river bridge into the cutting towards Llandarcy, we are starting to feel the climb, regulator is open to ¾, steam pressure drops back to 180 lb. I put the pricker in again, trying to clean the bars, the fire is starting to get a bit dirty with a few blue flames around. It seems to work and the pressure holds at 180 lb. water has dropped to ¼ glass, so the injector goes on. I inspect the fire with the shovel, guiding drafts of air into the box to see the fire. Finding a few low spots I at once fill these with coal and again put a few around the back end.

We are now passing the signal box at Jersey Marine Jn North and the engine is pounding into the climb, steam drops to below 180 lb. for the first time. I again put the pricker in and clear the bars, and then do a little light firing, it seems to do the trick and steam pressure returns to 180 lb. We pound into Llandarcy, we are given the loop signal here and run into the loop passing the outwards roads. We continue to climb over the top end of the inward sidings and stop clear of the top point of Llandarcy sidings where the trainmeeter detaches our brakevan near the box.

We descend into the oil refinery, pushing the tanks into the refinery sidings. The trainmeeter uncouples the vacuum pipes and the coupling and we pull forward and join our brake van in the loop. This was an unusual van, it was a Southern type with two bogies, we did not see many of them in this area. I went

'42XX' class 2-8-0T No. 5213 works into Briton Ferry yard *en route* to Llanelly.   *Norman Jones*

Llandarcy oil refinery complex. On the right is the refinery inward siding and bearing to the left is the Swansea Direct line to Briton Ferry.   *Author's Collection*

into the cabin to make a can of tea, the trainmeeter admiring our unusual locomotive. By this time I had worked the fire down reasonably low and had ¾ of water in the glass and 180 lb. pressure on the clock.

The driver went on the phone to control and he told me that we were not going to shed but a set of Eastern Depot men were going to relieve us there and take the engine to Landore shed. We had a 15 minute break then ran around our van in the loop and worked tender first down the bank to Jersey Marine Jn passing Jersey Marine yards, Burrows Sidings, Prince of Wales Dock Jn and onto Eastern Depot. When we got outside the shed a set of men came across and relieved us, we climbed down and booked off duty. Not a bad day all round, the 'Castle' not a bad engine but give us a '42XX' class anytime.

The 'Pembroke Coast Express' by Alan Ayres

When first introduced on 5th June, 1950, the 'Pembroke Coast Express' was billed as 'Wales' fastest train'. It left Pembroke Dock at 1.05 pm and ran to Swansea (High Street) arriving at 3.38 pm. Landore men would then work the train through to London (Paddington). This is the story of a typical trip with driver Harold Roliston and fireman Alan Ayres. Amongst the regular engines used on this and other London-bound expresses were Nos. 5010 *Restormel Castle*, 5039 *Rhuddlan Castle* (two particularly good performers), 7018 *Drysllwyn Castle* (now preserved at Didcot Railway Centre) and 7028 *Cadbury Castle*.

The Landore crew would book on at 1.45 pm and check the notices and then look at the duty sheet for their engine. After collecting our personal items from our lockers we would proceed to our booked engine, which usually stood on the No. 1 or 2 road on the shed. Once we had climbed aboard we would undo the locks on the footplate boxes. I would set off to the stores to draw some oil, and then set it on the side of the locomotive for my driver.

Once aboard I would check the water and fire, and test the sand pipes. Making my way to the front of the locomotive I would open the smokebox door and check the smokebox for fly ash and also check the boiler tubes for any sign of leaks. There was some cleaning to do on the footplate using an oily rag, and then wiping down the surfaces with clean waste. The fire would be built up at the front and back of the firebox with more at the back and around the sides. The paraffin wells would need to be filled in the lamps and the glasses cleaned.

The chargeman cleaner then came along with the 'Pembroke Coast Express' headboard and it would be placed on the front top lamp bracket. The vacuum pipe connection would be checked and the injectors tested. The cab floor would be gone over with paraffin and then washed down with the pep pipe.

When my mate finished oiling, the engine would pull forward to the water column to fill the tender. The water pressure would then be reduced to dampen down the coal dust in the tender. With preparations completed Harold would remove his prep overalls and put a clean set on.

The locomotive would then proceed to the shed board where I would then phone the signalman at Landore Station signal box. Once the signal was lowered the locomotive then proceeded onto the down road at Landore before

'Castle' class 4-6-0 No. 5013 *Abergavenny Castle* waits on the dock road at Swansea (High Street) to take over the 3.45 pm 'Pembroke Coast Express'.   *Norman Jones*

An unidentified 'Castle' class locomotive on the down 'Pembroke Coast Express' at Neath.
Norman Jones

we made our way to Swansea (High Street), via Loop East, the down relief line, the dock road and then onto the up main before running into the No. 1 bay and onto two coaches and a restaurant car. At about 3.20 pm the board would drop 'off' and we would pull out onto the up main line. The 1.05 pm from Pembroke Dock would then run into the platform. The dummy would show 'off' and we would back down towards the train, stopping about 3 ft away from it. The shunter would then set the buckeye coupling ready for impact and would then call us back and we would couple up, nine coaches on. The shunter would then give the 'blow up vacuum' signal and we gained 21 inches on the clock.

I now inspected the fire and again put coal around the back end as well as checking the front, putting in some coal on low areas. The boiler is ¾ full with steam at 200 lb., it is five minutes prior to departure. At 3.42 pm the signal is lowered and our road is set for departure. The engine blows off at 225 lb., the injector is on.

Departure time of 3.45 arrives and our guard gives us the 'right away' with his green flag. We reply with a whistle and pull away from the platform. The boiler is now full and the injector off, with steam at 210 lb. The firehole flap is up as we make our way up the incline to Hafod (Loop East) passing Landore shed. Running through Landore station we check our speed over the viaduct. Past the steelworks I start firing until we get to the flying arches at Lonlas. Passing Skewen East signal box and into Skewen station down the bank into Neath the injector is on and the engine blowing off.

Driver Harold Roliston checks our speed again through Neath station. Picking up the pace we pass Court Sart shed on our right-hand side. The boiler is full and the injector off as we run through Briton Ferry into Baglan Moors at around 50 mph. Our speed is checked approaching Port Talbot West crossing and Port Talbot station and we pass the goods yard and then on to Margam. All the distant signals are 'off' and once more we accelerate.

We are on the bank now, and I am firing continuously. The train is moving well but speed reduces as water drops to half a glass. The injector is on and we are holding steam at 200 lb. As we pass Pyle West signal box the regulator is at ¾ open and the engine is working hard. We maintain boiler pressure and I keep the back end of the fire up, firing lightly at the front end, ensuring the fire is clear of the brick arch. The signalman waves as we pass Pyle East and onto the last section of climb to Stormy Top. Boiler pressure drops to 180 lb. with ¾ of a glass of water and the injector off.

Once over the top I turn the injector back on, with the firehole flap down the steam pressure regains 200 lb. When the boiler is full I turn the injector off and running down the bank into Bridgend the engine blows off. We are doing 50 mph approaching Bridgend station and we check our speed for the curve after the platform into Tremains where there is a goods train in the loop.

With our boiler now full and the injector off we run at around 50 mph on the long straight before Pencoed. We check our speed for the station there as our engine blows off. I am firing continuously at this point as we climb towards Llanharan. The injector goes on as we pass Bryn-y-Gwinon crossing and pound through Llanharan station. The boiler pressure has dropped back to 180 lb. with the boiler ¾ full, I turn the injector off and the steam pressure holds as we pass Llanharan West signal box.

Once over the summit the boiler is down to half full and the injector turned on. We descend into Llantrisant past West signal box, through the station, and then around the curve over Miskin crossing as we pass two goods trains in the the long goods loop which are waiting for us to clear the section.

We pass St George's crossing at 50 mph and check our speed for the dip at Peterston. We proceed through St Fagan's and on to Ely. I stop firing and leave room in the boiler to allow for the Cardiff (General) station stop. Passing Cardiff (Canton) shed the boiler is half full with our pressure at 200 lb. Harold brakes as we approach Cardiff (General) and we pull to a stand at the end of the platform alongside the water column at 4.53 pm.

I climb onto the tender and Harold throws the chain over for me to pull the bag into the water hole on the tender. Harold turns the water on, while I go off to get a can of tea. By the time I get back, the tender tank is full and Harold has pulled the bag away and replaced the chain in the clip. I climb onto the tender and close the flap on the water filler hole and then get back onto the footplate.

There is a 'no smoke' rule at Cardiff (General) so there is no firing. We have seven minutes here. Meanwhile passengers get off and on, Post Office staff are putting mail onto the train. I keep the engine quiet with the injector on until the boiler is full. Just before departure the engine blows off. The guard and porters slam the carriage doors and then the guard whistles and shows us the green flag. I give the 'right away' to Harold and we pull away at 5.00 pm.

We head down the incline into Newtown and out through Pengam. I start firing again at Newtown and build up the fire, again filling the back end and peppering the front. At Marshfield I sit down with a cup of tea and a sandwich as we run into Ebbw Junction and then the Gaer tunnels before arriving at Newport station at 5.15 pm, one minute early.

I have left room in the boiler to keep the engine quiet in the platform, the firehole flap is down and the injector on. I water the coal in the tender, being careful not to get any water on the station platform. Pulling the coal forward and breaking up a few lumps, I trim the tender. We eventually get the 'right away' from the guard. The firehole flap is up and the boiler now full, the pressure reaches 225 lb. and the engine is blowing off. We draw away from the platform at 5.20 pm, on time.

We cross the large river bridge and then through East Usk goods yards. As we enter the long straight section past Llanwern I am firing again, building the fire up for the tunnel. We pass Magor and take water from the troughs at Undy. I lower the scoop and watch the gauge and once the tank is ¾ full the scoop is raised.

Running past the vast yards at Severn Tunnel Junction, a 'distant on' ATC bell rings caution. My mate cancels this out and checks his speed at Tunnel West and runs into Severn Tunnel Junction station at reduced speed. The distant for Severn Tunnel East is on here too and once more we have to check our speed.

I have room in the boiler to keep the engine quiet in the tunnel with the water level showing at ¾ of a glass. We run into the cutting approaching the tunnel with the blower on to keep the fumes out of the cab. The engine blows off and the injector is on as we enter the Severn tunnel. I drop the firehole flap as my mate checks our speed. The light from our fire makes the footplate look quite homely. Harold keeps the engine's regulator open to stop slipping. We reach the low point in the tunnel and begin to climb and my mate opens the regulator. I shut the injector off and close the firehole flap. We have 220 lb. of pressure and the engine climbs well to take us to Pilning. Fortunately we did not pass any other train in the tunnel so there is not too much smoke in our cab. On a bad day, especially with a banking engine, conditions would be very bad on the footplate leaving you unable to see your mate through the smoke.

We pounded out of Severn tunnel and through Pilning station and Patchway tunnel. I was firing again as I would be until we reached Filton Junction. There was 11 miles of bank to Filton and Stoke Gifford. The shovel is in constant use, with the injector on and pressure holding at 200 lb. The fire is quite extensive with a good back end and sides and a lower section down the front all white hot, the back end is not too heavy. I saw nothing of Winterbourne, Westerley or Wapley, it was just plain thrashing all the way to Sodbury tunnel. We passed through the centre road at Chipping Sodbury before lowering our scoop to refill the tender from the troughs just before Sodbury tunnel. In the tunnel the injector is on and the boiler pressure drops to 180 lb., but we emerge from the tunnel and run into Badminton.

The boiler pressure rises to 200 lb. with the firehole flap down. I am still firing as we descend the bank through the short tunnel at Alderton and then through Hullavington and Little Somerford before the slight rise to Brinkworth and then the drop into Wootton Bassett. Here we look out for the distant signal, we are travelling at around 60 mph and I am still firing. We pass Rushey Platt Junction and on through Swindon. If the distant signal was 'off' for Swindon Middle you would have the road through to Stratton Park and on to Shrivenham.

We looked out for the distant signal at Uffington and then continued through Wantage Road. After Steventon where we watched out for another distant signal, we rocked over the crossing at 60 mph through Milton. The distant signal was 'off' for Foxhall Junction and we proceeded through Didcot station, from here to Paddington we have quadruple track. We now look out for the distant signal at Moreton Cutting, and next the distant signal at Goring.

My mate says, 'Troughs coming up'. We take on more water, lower the scoop, fill the tank, then raise the scoop. If the distant signal had been 'on' at Goring we would have been unable to take water as you need to be travelling at around 50 mph. In that instance we would have had to whistle up at Pangbourne signal box that we required water at Reading station. There are intermediate block sections either side of Pangbourne and we look out for the distant signal at Tilehurst as we run parallel with the River Thames.

Onto Reading West Jn we steam, and through the middle road at Reading station at 60 mph before tearing through Sonning cutting, Twyford and Ruscombe. I stop firing at Slough and watch out for signals at Southall, where colour light signals start. Onwards through Hanwell Bridge, West Ealing, we are doing 80 mph through Ealing Broadway.

At Ealing I shut off the injector to leave room in the boiler for our time at Paddington. Through Old Oak Common my mate checks our speed and at Kensal Green we get a signal check, the ATC bell rings caution and my mate puts the brakes on. We run through Royal Oak. He again checks our speed at Ranelagh Bridge, then releases his brakes and opens up for the slight climb into Paddington. We come to a stop just short of the buffers on platform 4 at about 7.40

0-6-0PT No. 6410 arrives at Quaker's Yard with an Aberdare to Pontypool Road passenger service.

S. Rickard

Pannier tank No. 6437 of Aberdare shed has just taken water at Neath prior to leaving with a Vale of Neath train to Aberdare.

Norman Jones

pm. We have five minutes recovery time on timetable, official time of arrival is 7.45 pm. Pressure has dropped to 180 lb. with the boiler ¾ full and the injector on. I sweep up the footplate and then put the pricker through the fire to inspect it.

I finsh the last of my tea and sit down and wait for movement. We lock our tools away in the box on the footplate and set lamps right for shed. With a pilot on the rear end (now leading), the pilot's driver gives a crow on the whistle and we quietly slide out of the platform for Old Oak Common sidings. We are uncoupled there and then proceed into Old Oak Common shed and onto the pit road. Harold reports any faults to the fitter. My mate finishes his reports and gives them to the time clerk and we then make our way to the hostel. By 9.00 pm we are in the canteen for supper.

We put in a call for 5.30 am. After a bite for breakfast in the canteen we book on at 7.15 am for the 8.55 am Paddington to Swansea 'South Wales Pullman'. We prepare our engine, the same one we had the day before, and then make a can of tea before leaving the shed at about 8.15 am. We follow the empty coaches from the sidings into Paddington and join our coaches in the platform. I couple up and put on the lamps for 'right away' at 8.55 am and we arrive back in Swansea at around 1.25 pm.

The end of passenger services on the Vale of Neath Line by Brian Dodson

The final day of passenger working on the Vale of Neath line was 13th June, 1964. Swansea crews manned prairie tank No. 4108 and pannier tank No. 4612 which were to work between Swansea (High Street) and Neath (General) on that day.

Prairie tank No. 4110 was prepared at Court Sart shed before making its way to Neath (General) station in readiness to work the 7.40 am to Pontypool Road. At Pontllanfraith (Low Level) No. 4110 and its train passed pannier tank No. 4639 which was hauling the first passenger train of the day from Pontypool Road to Neath (the 8.40 am). No. 4110 arrived at Pontypool Road at 9.44 am and her crew had just over an hour to attend to the locomotive's needs before returning to Neath with the 11.00 am service.

The 'Vale' auto train in the platform at Neath in 1954. '56XX' class 0-6-2T No. 5656 is on the centre road.   *Norman Jones*

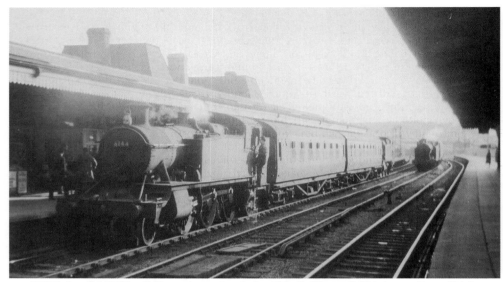

'61XX' class 2-6-2T No. 6144 couples up to a train at Neath (General). This locomotive will take the train on to Swansea. '51XX' class 2-6-2T No. 4110 is at the opposite end of the train having worked in over the Vale of Neath line. In the middle road stands '56XX' class 0-6-2T No. 6690.

Robert Thomas

'51XX' class 2-6-2T No. 4142 leaves Neath (General) with a train for Pontypool Road.

Norman Jones

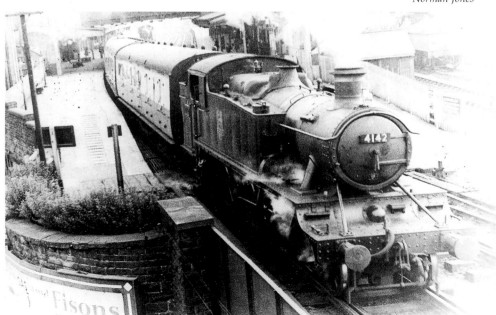

BR Standard 2-6-4T class '4MT' No. 80133 passes through Neath Junction with a Pontypool Road- Neath train with the Klondyke siding to the left and the Swansea siding to the right.
Robert Thomas

No. 80133 leaves Neath with a Swansea train. *Robert Thomas*

PONTYPOOL ROAD, CARDIFF, ABERDARE, NEATH and SWANSEA

WEEK DAYS ONLY

Miles from Pontypool Rd.	Station		am 2		am	am 2	am		am 2		am		am 2	am E		am J S		pm S 2	pm S 2		pm	
	164Newport	dep	..	..	..	..	7 3	..	..	..	8 3	..	..	10 3	..	10 3	..	..	..	..	12 3	..
—	**Pontypool Road**	dep	Workmen's Train	..	..	..	**7 38**	..	..	..	8 40	..	..	11 0	..	11 0	..	..	..	..	1 0	..
1¼	Pontypool **A**	..		..	..	..	7 43	..	..	..	8 45	..	..	11 4	..	11 4	..	..	..	..	1 5	..
5¼	Hafodyrynys Platform	..		..	..	..	..	..	..	..	8 59	..	..	11 18	..	11 18	..	..	..	..	1 19	..
6¼	Crumlin (High Level)	..		..	..	..	8 1	..	..	..	9 5	..	..	11 24	..	11 24	..	..	..	..	1 25	..
7¾	Pentwyn nawr Platform	..		..	..	..	..	..	..	..	..	..	..	..	..	..	..	..	..	..	..	..
9	Pontllanfraith (L.L.)	..		..	..	..	8 9	..	..	..	9 13	..	..	11 32	..	11 32	..	..	..	..	1 32	..
11	Hengoed (H.L.) **D**	arr		..	..	..	8 13	..	..	..	9 17	..	..	11 36	..	11 36	..	..	..	..	1 36	..
—	Mls **Cardiff** (Q.St.)	dep	5 15	..	..	6‡35	..	..	**8 15**	..	**8 15**	..	..	**10 58**	..	**10 58**	..	..	..	..	**1 0**	..
—	12½ Ystrad Mynach	..	5 47	..	..	7 23	..	..	8 48	..	8 48	..	..	11 31	..	11 31	..	1237	..	..	1 33	..
—	13½ Hengoed (L.L.) **F**	arr	5 49	..	..	..	..	..	8 50	..	8 50	..	..	11 34	..	11 34	..	..	..	..	1 35	..
—	Hengoed (H.L.)	dep	6 10	..	..	..	8 15	..	8 58	..	9 19	..	..	11 37	..	11 37	..	..	..	..	1 39	..
14	**Nelson and Llancaiach**	arr	**6 16**	..	..	**7 30**	**8 21**	..	**9 4**	..	**9 25**	..	..	**11 43**	..	**11 43**	..	**1242**	..	..	**1 45**	..
		dep	**6 17**	..	..	**7 33**	**8 22**	..	..	..	**9 26**	..	**9 35**	**11 44**	..	**11 44**	..	**1249**	..	..	**1 46**	..
14¾	Trelewis Halt	..	To Dowlais (Cae Harris), arr 6 53 am (Table 139)	..	..	7 36	8 25	..	..	..	9 28	..	To Dowlais (Cae Harris) arr 10 7 am (Table 139)	11 47	..	11 47	..	To Dowlais (Cae Harris) arr 1 25 pm (Table 139)	..	..	1 49	..
15½	Treharris	..		..	..	7 40	8 28	..	..	..	9 31	..		11 50	..	11 50	..		..	..	1 52	..
16	**Quaker's Yd.** (H.L.) **G**	arr		..	..	**7 43**	**8 30**	..	..	..	**9 33**	..		**11 52**	..	**11 52**	..		..	..	**1 54**	..
22¾	125Merthyr ¶	arr		..	..	8 15	8 57	..	..	..	10 45	..		12 42	..	12 42	..		..	..	2 42	..
—	**Quaker's Yd.** (H.L.)	dep		..	..	**7 45**	**8 33**	..	..	..	**9 36**	..		**11 55**	..	**11 55**	..		**1 12**	..	**1 57**	..
17¾	Penrhiwceiber (H.L.)	..		..	..	7 52	8 39	..	..	..	9 41	..		12 0	..	12 0	..		1 17	..	2 3	..
19	Mountain Ash (Cardiff Rd.)	..		..	..	7 56	8 43	..	..	..	9 45	..		12 4	..	12 4	..		1 21	..	2 6	..
21½	Cwmbach Halt	..		..	..	8 0	8 47	..	..	..	9 49	..		12 8	..	12 8	..		1 25	..	2 10	..
22¾	**Aberdare (H.L.)**	arr		..	..	**8 4**	**8 51**	..	..	..	**9 53**	..		**12 13**	..	**12 13**	..		**1 30**	..	**2 15**	..
		dep		..	**7 5**	**8 5**	..	..	..	..	**9 58**	..		**12 16**	..	**12 19**	..		..	..	**2 16**	..
23¾	Trecynon Halt	..		..	7 8	8 8	..	..	..	..	..	..		..	..	..	..		..	..	2 20	..
26½	Hirwaun	arr		..	7 15	8 15	..	..	..	..	10 6	..		12 24	..	12 27	..		..	..	2 25	..
—		dep	..	..	7 16	8 16	..	..	..	..	10 7	..	..	12 26	..	12 29	..	..	..	..	2 26	..
28½	Rhigos Halt	..	..	..	7 23	8 21	..	..	..	..	..	..	..	..	..	..	..	..	..	..	2 30	..
31	Pontwalby Halt	..	..	..	..	8 29	..	..	..	..	..	..	..	..	..	..	..	..	..	..	2 38	..
32¾	Glyn Neath	..	..	..	7 40	8 34	..	..	..	..	10 23	..	..	12 42	..	12 45	..	..	..	..	2 43	..
35¾	Resolven	..	..	..	7 46	8 40	..	..	..	..	10 29	..	..	12 48	..	12 52	..	..	..	..	2 49	..
36¾	Melyncourt Halt	..	..	..	..	8 43	..	..	..	..	..	..	..	..	..	..	..	..	..	..	2 52	..
37¾	Clyne Halt	..	..	..	..	8 46	..	..	..	..	..	..	..	..	..	..	..	..	..	..	2 56	..
40	Aberdylais Halt	..	..	..	7 54	8 51	..	..	..	..	..	..	..	12 57	..	1 1	..	..	..	..	3 1	..
41½	**Neath (General)**	arr	..	..	**7 58**	8L55	..	..	..	..	**10 40**	..	..	**1 1**	..	**1 5**	..	..	..	..	**3 5**	..
49½	**104Swansea** (H. St.)	arr	..	..	**8 35**	9§40	..	..	..	..	**11 5**	..	..	**2 26**	..	**1 46**	..	..	..	..	**3T55**	..

The Vale of Neath timetable 9th September, 1963 to 14th June, 1964.

PONTYPOOL ROAD, CARDIFF, ABERDARE, NEATH and SWANSEA
WEEK DAYS ONLY

	pm	pm E ②		pm S ②		pm J			pm ②		pm ②			pm ②			pm			pm			pm S ②		pm S ②	
164 Newport .. .. dep	1 5	..		..		2 46	..	..	4 3	..		②	..		②	..		..	..	..	8 15	..		②	..	②	..
Pontypool Road ... dep	2 25					3 55	..		5 0												8 55						
Pontypool A ...	2 30					4 0			5 5												9 0						
Hafodyrynys Platform ...	2 44																				9 14						
Crumlin (High Level) ...	2 50					4 18	..		5 24												9 20						
Pentwynmawr Plat'orm...																											
Pontllanfraith (L.L.)f ..	2 57					4 26			5 32												9 27						
Hengoed (H.L.) D .... arr	3 1					4 30			5 36												9 31						
Cardiff (Q.St.) .. dep	2 0		Workmen's Train	2‡40		3 40			5 0	5‡ 0		5 20			6 15			8 30			9‡30					1055	
Ystrad Mynach				3 17		4 18			5 34	5 43		5 53			6 49			9 3			10 7					1127	
Hengoed (L.L.) F arr	2 36					4 20			5 36			5 55			6 51			9 5								1129	
Hengoed (H.L.)...... dep	3 3					4 33			5 39			6 5			7 0			9 33								1143	
Nelson and Llancaiach { arr	3 9			3 22		4 40			5 45	5 48		6 11			7 7			9 39			1012					1150	
{ dep	3 10	3 15		3 27		4 42			5 46	5 52		6 12			7 8			9 40			1017					1154	
Trelewis Halt	3 13					4 45			5 49			6 14			7 10			9 43									
Treharris	3 16					4 49			5 52			6 17			7 13			9 46									
Quaker's Yd. (H.L.) G arr	3 18					4 51			5 54			6 19			7 15			9 48									
125 Merthyr ¶ ...... arr	3 42					5 20			6 53			6 53			7 42			1042									
Quaker's Yd. (H.L.). dep	3 21		Cae Harris (Table 139)		Cae Harris (Table 139)	4 56			5 57		Cae Harris (Table 139)	6 22			7 19			9 49		Cae Harris (Table 139)			Cae Harris (Table 139)				
Penrhiwceiber (H.L.)			To Dowlais		To Dowlais	5 2			6 3		To Dowlais	6 27			7 24			9 55		To Dowlais			To Dowlais				
Mountain Ash (Cardiff Rd.)	3 32		arr 3 52 pm		arr 4 0 pm	5 5			6 7		arr 6 28 pm	6 31			7 28			9 59		arr 10 48 pm			arr 12 27 am				
Cwmbach Halt	3 36					5 9			6 11			6 35			7 33			10 4									
Aberdare (H.L.) .. { arr	3 42					5 13			6 15			6 40			7 38			10 9									
{ dep	3 51					5 18																					
Trecynon Halt	3 55					5 22																					
Hirwaun .... { arr	4 0					5 27																					
{ dep	4 5					5 30																					
Rhigos Halt						5 36																					
Pontwalby Halt........																											
Glyn Neath	4 21					5 48																					
Resolven	4 27					5 54																					
Melyncourt Halt																											
Clyne Halt																											
Aberdylais Halt	4 36																										
Neath (General) .... arr	4 40					6 8																					
104 Swansea (H. St.) . arr	5B24					6 34																					

A Clarence Street
B On Saturdays arr 5 53 pm
D Adjoins Hengoed (L.L.) Station
E Except Saturdays
F Adjoins Hengoed High Level Station
G Adjoins Quaker's Yard Low Level Station
J Through train Pontypool Road to Swansea (H.St.)

L Arr Neath (Riverside) Station Mondays to Fridays
p pm
S or S Saturdays only
T On Saturdays arr 3 33 pm
‡ Change at Ystrad Mynach

§ On Mondays to Fridays passengers make their own way between Neath (Riverside) end Neath (General). On Saturdays arr Swansea (H. St.) 9 26 am
¶ Passengers change from High Level to Low Level at Quaker's Yard
② Second class only

LOCAL TRAINS and Intermediate Stations between Cardiff and Hengoed (L.L.), see Table 131

OTHER TRAINS between Cardiff and Quaker's Yard, see Table 125—Penrhiwceiber and Abardare Table 127

The Vale of Neath timetable 9th September, 1963 to 14th June, 1964.

SWANSEA, NEATH, ABERDARE, CARDIFF and PONTYPOOL ROAD

WEEK DAYS ONLY

Miles	Station		am (2)	am (2)	am (2)	am	am	am	am	noon (2)	am	pm E (2)	pm S (2)
—	104Swansea (H. St.)	dep	..	..	..	..	..	7 20	..	..	10 20	..	..
7½	**Neath** (General)	dep						7 40			11 5		
9¼	Aberdylais Halt		..	..	..	..	..	7 48	..	..	11 12	..	..
11¾	Clyne Halt												
12¾	Melyncourt Halt		..	..	..	..	..	..	..	..	..	..	..
13½	Resolven							7 56			11 20		
16½	Glyn Neath		..	..	..	..	..	8 3	..	..	11 27	..	..
18½	Pontwalby Halt							8 8					
21¼	Rhigos Halt		..	..	..	..	..	..	..	..	..	..	..
23¼	Hirwaun	arr						8 22			11 44		
		dep						8 25			11 49		
25¾	Trecynon Halt			..		..	..	8 31	..		11 55		
26¾	**Aberdare** (H.L.)	arr						8 34			11 59		
		dep		6 24		7 45	8 5	8 35	11 0		12 2		
28¼	Cwmbach Halt			6 28		7 49	8 9	8 39	11 4		12 6		
30½	Mountain Ash (Cardiff Rd.)			6 32		7 55	8 14	8 44	11 9		12 11		
31¾	Penrhiwceiber (H.L.)			6 36		7 59	8 18	8 48	1113		12 15		
33½	**Quaker's Yd.** (H.L.) **G**	arr		6 41		8 5	8 23	8 53	1119		12 20		
—	125Merthyr ¶	dep	Dep Dowlais (Cae Harris) 5 20 am (Table 139)	5 55	Dep Dowlais (Cae Harris) 7 38 am (Table 139)	7 25	8 0	8 23	11 0	Dep Dowlais (Cae Harris) 11 32 am (Table 139)	12 0	Dep Dowlais (Cae Harris) 1 15 pm (Table 139)	Dep Dowlais (Cae Harris) 1 55 pm (Table 139)
—	**Quaker's Yd.** (H.L.)	dep		6 42		8 7	8 24	8 54	1122		12 21		
34½	Treharris			6 44		8 9	8 27	8 56	1125		12 24		
34¾	Trelewis Halt			6 47		8 12	8 30	8 59	1128		12 27		
35½	**Nelson and Llancaiach**	arr	5 49	6 49	8 6	8 14	8 32	9 1	1130	12 0	12 29	1 48	2 20
		dep	5 54	6 50	8 7	8 15	8 33	9 2	1131	12 2	12 30		2 22
38½	Hengoed (H.L.) **D**	arr	6 1		8 14	8 22		9 8	1138		12 37		
—	Mls Hengoed (L.L.)	dep	6 4	..	8 17	..	..	1013	1214	..	12 53	Workmen's Train	..
—	1 Ystrad Mynach		6 7	6 55	8 20		8 39	1016	1217	12 7	12 56		2 27
—	13½ **Cardiff** (Q. St.)	arr	6 38	7‡30	8 51	..	9‡14	1047	1248	12‡48	1 28		3‡ 6
—	Hengoed (H.L.)	dep				8 30		9 9	1140		12 38		
40½	Pontllanfraith (L.L.)			..	..	8 34	..	9 13	1145	..	12 42		..
41½	Pentwynmawr Platform												
43¼	Crumlin (H.L.)		Workmen's Train	..	..	8 42	..	9 21	1152	..	12 50	..	..
44	Hafodyrynys Platform					8 48					12 56		
48½	Pontypool **A**			..	..	9 1	..	9 40	1211	..	1 10	..	..
49½	**Pontypool Road**	arr				9 5		9 44	1215		1 18		
59½	164Newport	arr		..	..	9 42	..	1115	1 0	..	2 4	..	..

The Vale of Neath timetable 9th September, 1963 to 14th June, 1964.

SWANSEA, NEATH, ABERDARE, CARDIFF and PONTYPOOL ROAD

WEEK DAYS ONLY

Columns marked **E②**, **S②**, **S②**, **S②** carry trains **Dep Dowlais (Cae Harris)** at **4 15 pm**, **4 55 pm**, **9 15 pm** and **11 3 pm** respectively (Table 139).

Station	pm	pm E ②	pm J ②	pm S ②	pm H ②	pm F ②	pm S ②	pm J ②	pm S ②	pm EY	pm SJ ②	pm S ②
184 Swansea (H. St.) dep			2 55		3 45	3 45	3 45	5 25		8 45	8 45	
Neath (General) dep			3 26		4L20	4L20	4 27	5 56		9 10	9 10	
Aberdylais Halt			3 31		4 24	4 24	4 31					
Clyne Halt					4 30	4 30	4 37					
Melyncourt Halt					4 33	4 33	4 40					
Resolven			3 41		4 37	4 37	4 43	6 9		9 22	9 22	
Glyn Neath			3 50		4 44	4 44	4 50	6 17		9 29	9 29	
Pontwalby Halt					4 49	4 49	4 55					
Rhigos Halt			4 12		4 58	5 4	5 5					
Hirwaun arr			4 18		5 4	5 12	5 10	6 35		9 47	9 47	
Hirwaun dep			4 19		5 6	5 14	5 14	6 38		9 49	9 49	
Tracynon Halt			4 24		5 11	5 19	5 20			9 55	9 55	
Aberdare (H.L.) arr			4 28		5 16	5 24	5 24	6 45		10 1	10 1	
Aberdare (H.L.) dep	3 50		4 33		5 20	5 25	5 27	6 50			10 5	
Cwmbach Halt	3 54		4 38		5 24	5 29	5 31	6 55			10 9	
Mountain Ash (Cardiff Rd.)	3 58		4 43		5 29	5 34	5 36	7 0			10 14	
Penrhiwceiber (H.L.)	4 2		4 48		5 33	5 38	5 40	7 4			10 18	
Quaker's Yd. (H.L.) G arr	4 7		4 55		5 38	5 43	5 45	7 10			10 23	
125 Merthyr ¶ dep	3 0		4 0		5 0	5 0	5 0	6 25			10 0	
Quaker's Yd. (H.L.) dep	4 8		4 59		5 39	5 44	5 46	7 12			10 24	
Treharris	4 11		5 2		5 42	5 46	5 49	7 15			10 27	
Trelewis Halt	4 13		5 5		5 44	5 49	5 51	7 18			10 30	
Nelson and Llancaiach arr	4 15	4 43	5 8	5 20	5 46	5 51	5 53	7 20	9 40		10 33	11 28
Nelson and Llancaiach dep	4 16	4 45	5 10	5 22	5 47	5 52	5 54	7 22	9 45		10 34	11 29
Hengoed (H.L.) D arr	4 23		5 17		5 54	5 59	6 1	7 29			10 40	11 36
Hengoed (L.L.) dep	4 28		5 24		6 15	6 15	6 15	7 39				
Ystrad Mynach	4 31	4 51	5 28	5 28	6 18	6 18		7 42	9 50			
Cardiff (Q. St.) arr	5 6	5‡25	5 58		6 49	6 49		8 15	10‡49			
Hengoed (H.L.) dep	4 32		5 21					7 30			10 41	
Pontllanfraith (L.L.)	4 36		5 26					7 34			10 47	
Pentwynmawr Platform	4E39											
Crumlin (H.L.)	4 44		5 34					7 41			10 54	
Hafodyrynys Platform	4 50		5 40								11 0	
Pontypool A	5 4		5 54					8 0			11 14	
Pontypool Road arr	5 10		5 58					8 4			11 18	
164 Newport arr	6 8		7 55					9 9			11 43	

A Clarence Street
D Adjoins Hengoed (L.L.) Station
E Except Saturdays
F Fridays only
G Adjoins Quaker's Yard Low Level Station

H Mondays to Thursdays inclusive
J Through train Swansea (H.St.) to Pontypool Road
L Neath (Riverside) Station
S or S Saturdays only
Y Through train Swansea (H. St.) to Aberdare (H.L.)

‡ Change at Ystrad Mynach
¶ Passengers change from Low Level to High Level at Quaker's Yard
② Second class only

LOCAL TRAINS and intermediate Stations between Hengoed (L.L.) and Cardiff, see Table 131

OTHER TRAINS between Aberdare and Penrhiwceiber, see Table 127—Quaker's Yard and Cardiff Table 125

The Vale of Neath timetable 9th September, 1963 to 14th June, 1964.

'51XX' class 2-6-2T No. 4110 on the 11.00 am Pontypool Road to Neath at Trecynon on 13th June, 1964.   *T. Williams Collection*

'Grange' class 4-6-0 No. 6836 *Estevarney Grange* running down the bank with the 5.56 pm from Neath at Trecynon on 13th June, 1964.   *T. Williams Collection*

No. 4639 had arrived at Neath at 10.40 am and she had just 25 minutes there before setting off once more with the 11.05 am to Pontypool Road. This train was passed near Mountain Ash by No. 4110 at the head of the 11.00 am from Pontypool Road, a through train to Swansea (High Street). Near Pontypool No. 4639 then passed the 1 pm from Pontypool Road hauled by pannier tank No. 9609 which was to arrive at Neath (General) at 3.05 pm. No. 4639's arrival time at Pontypool Road was 1.18 pm, her return working was to be the 3.55 pm.

Larger motive power was in evidence on the 2.25 pm from Pontypool Road in the form of 'Grange' class 4-6-0 No. 6836 *Estevarney Grange*. This train arrived at Neath at 4.40 pm. *Estevarney Grange* returning at the head of the 5.56 pm, arriving back at Pontypool Road at 8.04 pm.

The next engine to put an appearance in on the final day was 2-6-2T No. 4121 which hauled the 3.26 pm from Neath arriving at Pontypool Road at 5.58 pm. No. 4121 had passed the 3.55 pm through train from Pontypool Road to Swansea (High Street) at Quaker's Yard. No. 4639 only worked the 3.55 pm train as far as Neath. No. 4121's final working of the day was to be the 8.55 pm from Pontypool Road to Aberdare (High Level).

No. 4639's train arrived at 6.08 pm at Neath (General). The engine then ran light engine to Court Sart shed for servicing as the engine had been working since 8.40 am when it first departed from Pontypool Road. The Neath shed staff took the opportunity to clean the engine and apply some fresh paint to smarten up the locomotive for the final passenger working over the Vale of Neath line.

No. 4639 departed Neath (General) at 9.10 pm with the last timetabled passenger train over the Vale of Neath line. She arrived at Pontypool Road at 11.18 pm and when the locomotive had its fire dropped on Pontypool Road shed later that night it signalled the end of an era.

Neath shed staff have 'bulled up' 0-6-0PT No. 4639. It is seen waiting to depart from Neath (General) with the last train, the 9.10 pm from Neath on 13th June, 1964.

R. Thomas

Freight traffic continued over the Vale of Neath line after closure to passengers. Class '37' No. 37251 stands with two National Coal Board locomotives at Aberpergwm colliery prior to working the final train from the colliery to the washery at Wernos on the Central Wales line on 13th May, 1985.   *Author*

The last train for Wernos washery to leave the Vale of Neath line approaches Neath & Brecon Junction signal box. The signalman waits to retrieve the 'one train working' staff.   *Author*

Class '37' No. 37428 with a weedkiller train at Aberpergwm sidings in 1987.   *Author*

Aberpergwm colliery after closure in 1985.   *Author*

A class '66' pulls down from the coaling plant at Cwmgrwach on the Vale of Neath line on 28th
September, 2003. *D. Llewellyn*

Class '66' No. 66220 with empties at the new disposal site in Cwmgrwach on 28th September,
2003. Cwmgrwach plant was 'moth balled' in 2007. *D. Llewellyn*

Chapter Seven

Other People's Memories

My 47 years of Railway Service (by John Last of Neath)

I joined the railway on 3rd May, 1954, when my father took me to see Mr Stan Jones, the shedmaster at the Neath & Brecon shed in Cadoxton, Neath. Mr Jones arranged for me to go to Swindon for a cleaner's examination at Park House, where all the footplate staff went. The morning consisted of a full medical, eyesight test and a medical questionnaire. In the afternoon if the medical was satisfactory we would then see the safety inspector who would talk us through our duties and give us a brief outline of our movement through the grades. Next we went to the uniform stores to kit us out in overalls and a grease top cap, and were told to report to the shed master at Neath & Brecon shed on Monday morning at 9.00 am.

On that first day Mr Jones took me around the shed and indicated what my duties were, showed me around an engine pointing out the different aspects of my work, he then took me to meet the shed staff. I was told to report at 9.00 am on the Tuesday to start my cleaning duties. There were four cleaners on duty, but some of these could be out covering holiday or sickness on pilot duties, so there might only be two of us on shed at any one time.

On Tuesday I was instructed to carry out my duties in a confident manner because if the engine was not cleaned properly the driver would complain, especially the motions where the driver had to go to do most of his oiling, and if his overalls got dirty he would play hell. Part of our duties was calling out drivers on early mornings. One morning I went to call a driver at Cadoxton and knocked at the wrong house; the people concerned were furious and I had a dressing down from Mr Jones when I went back. So my duties as a cleaner had begun.

In August 1955, I was sent for a test to go out firing and passed. I went into the Pilot link and worked duties on Neath N&B yard and Neath Jn and remained in this link for about 18 months. One of the duties on the N&B yard pilot was shunting the Cadoxton Brewery and if you were lucky the driver would allow you to have a glass of beer. He would have considerably more than that himself! That duty also brought traffic over for the seed store in the old goods shed, also the odd sand wagon for the shed. The cleaners would be asked to unload this wagon into the sand house, but this work was very hard and long and you had a job to finish. Also we brought the brewery traffic over which consisted of grain and coal for the boilers, taking out loaded vans to be marshalled into trains to travel to destination.

When I started as a cleaner my wages were under £3 a week, a fireman's was about £7 10s. and a driver's about £12 on a 48 hour week, but you could get a pint for a shilling in those days.

The work on the Pilots was very straightforward, there were three turns round the clock on the Neath Jn Pilot, Target 4 finishing at 8.00 pm when the

Footplate crew Glyn John and John Last with the guard and signalman at Ynysdawley signal
box.   *John Last*

engine went to shed. Neath N&B Yard Target 5 started at 6.30 am and comprised two shifts, to 10.00 pm Mondays to Fridays, Saturdays were from 6.30 am to 8.0 pm. Duties on the T4 included shunting at Neath Jn and tripping to Neath station with transfer traffic. The N&B Yard T5 duties consisted of making up trains for the branch (empties) and forming traffic for Swansea Docks, also shunting the new siding and moving coaches to and from the Riverside station. Sometimes empties came from Swansea Docks with an Eastern Depot man who would not go to the bone yard with empties as he did not know the road, and we would have to take the train from the station to Cadoxton sidings.

I eventually moved into No. 2 link after about 18 months and took on train work, although I had been on these duties covering sickness and holiday relief so I knew how to handle train work. My mate was Harold Davies for some years who was a very good driver, easy on the regulator and an all-round good driver. When on banking duties the front engine driver used to complain that he did not do his fair share of pushing; he would say he was looking after his fireman. There were 12 sets of men in No. 2 link and it was all mineral work taking empties to the collieries and coal back for Swansea Docks and other destinations. Some of the drivers were very heavy on the regulator and you would have to work much harder with these drivers. I was caught out when my mate Harold went on holiday and I was with a heavy driver. I was firing as normal but due to the fire disappearing up the chimney much faster, some areas of the grate became low and started to draw air. My steam pressure went back and I started to fill the box with coal to compensate but put too much on and we stuck for steam at Cilfrew on a goods train. But this was a learning curve and we did have our problems from time to time.

On the return trip we would take coal down the branch to Neath N&B Yard. Some drivers could work the train spot on and be able to run from Onllwyn to Neath and others would use the regulator most of the way because of having too many brakes down. On some occasions the train was unable to get away and the guard would have to walk down and pick a few brakes up for the train to get away, resetting them afterwards. The form was that when the driver pulled away from the colliery the guard pinned down brakes until the driver felt he had enough brakes down, he then blew two on the whistle and proceeded down the branch. The more cautious drivers would have more brakes down than the more confident drivers, with these drivers you could run to Neath with your existing fire which was quite large by the time you got to Onllwyn and put the empties in the colliery. With the nervous drivers you would have to fire all the way to Neath.

When working bunker first down the bank you had to keep the coal well watered because the dust would blow into the cab, the driver would soon tell you if you did not carry out this operation. The running time from Onllwyn was approximately 60 minutes and the speed would be about 12 mph. We would change tokens at Ynysdawley, Crynant, Cilfrew, Cadoxton and at Neath N&B Yard we handed in our token to the signalman.

There was a period when the coal traffic at Onllwyn was on stop due to a problem with the new open cast site, and for a short time we were booking on and off and getting a day's pay. I lost my mate when he moved into No. 1

BRITISH RAILWAYS - WESTERN REGION

NOTICE TO STAFF.

A.S.L.E. & F. STRIKE

You will have seen the notice published by the British Transport Commission, which sets out very clearly the facts surrounding the circumstances which led to the recent decision of the A.S.L.E. & F., to withdraw the labour of their members as from Saturday midnight, 28th May, and gives particulars of the offer made by the Commission.

Do you know what the offer means to the Staff? The following are examples of the combined effect of the train allowance and mileage proposals.

Drivers engaged regularly on train work involving a daily mileage of -	Additional weekly payment (Train allowance plus mileage)	
	Group 1. (A.C. & D. Trains)	Group 2 (all other trains)
80 miles and under	5/-	2/6
90 miles	6/4½	3/10½
100 "	7/9	5/3
110 "	9/1½	6/7½
120 "	10/6	8/-
130 "	11/10½	9/4½
140 "	13/3	10/9

above 140 - Present mileage arrangements will continue to apply but all Drivers of Group 1 and Group 2 trains would, in addition, receive the proposed train allowance of 5/- and 2/6 per week respectively.

Firemen engaged regularly on train work involving a daily mileage of -	Additional weekly payment (for mileage)
80 miles and under	
90 miles	1/2
100 "	2/3½
110 "	3/5
120 "	4/7
130 "	5/9
140 "	6/10½

above 140 - Present mileage arrangements will continue to apply.

I APPEAL TO ALL FOOTPLATE STAFF TO RETURN TO WORK, AND SO MAINTAIN THE GOOD NAME OF FOOTPLATE STAFF AND NOT JEOPARDISE THE INDUSTRY FROM WHICH WE ALL OBTAIN OUR LIVELIHOOD.

H.E.A. WHITE

MOTIVE POWER SUPERINTENDENT.

30th May, 1955.

passenger link and for a time I had to work with different drivers when I realised the different standards of driving.

In 1955 we went on strike and I was on picket duties. Two our drivers would not strike, but one went on the sick but Aubrey Bracey came to work and was deemed to be a blackleg. We worked picket duties for two hour shifts throughout the day and night, this went on for 17 days until the strike was resolved. When the strike was over the men would not talk to Aubrey, it was very difficult. Then I was put with him for a short time and on the first day I made a decision that it would make my job very hard if we could not work together, so I said to Aubrey that I had made my mind up to forget the past and to improve the ongoing situation we should work together in harmony and he was pleased with that. Although Aubrey was a heavy driver he taught me many tricks of the trade and we got on well together.

I eventually moved up to No. 1 link and with some surprise I was with my old mate Harold and stayed with him until he retired. There was one old driver, Harry Box, who was most peculiar. One trip that comes to mind was when we were working the Abercrave and stopped for food. He got out from his food box two kippers and they were 'humming'; he held them in front of the open fire and warmed them up, the smell was foul and I had to take my food off the engine and sit on the grass to escape the smell. I will never forget that time; I don't like kippers, who can blame me?

In the passenger link one turn in the morning was the 6.00 am colliers train from Neath Riverside to Colbren and return with the 8.10 am passenger from Colbren. There was also a 6.35 am colliers from Colbren to Riverside, the outward working on this turn was the 4.15 am goods from Neath N&B Yard which arrived at Colbren at 5.39 am. There was also a 3.0 pm colliers from Colbren. The only through train we worked to Brecon in my time was the 4.10 pm from Riverside which arrived in Brecon at 5.51 pm. The back working was the 6.20 pm Brecon arriving in Neath Riverside at 7.54 pm. Our late turn was the 9.40 pm passenger from Riverside to Colbren, returning with the 12.05 am Onllwyn Goods.

The other through Brecon train was 8.25 am on Saturday mornings, we worked this duty to Craig-y-Nos and changed over with the Brecon men at this point, working back from Craig-y-Nos with the Brecon train to Neath Riverside.

It was fascinating when you changed drivers and had to change your firing techniques to suit their different way of driving. Driver Dai Hopkins ('Dai mate') always had a fag in his mouth, but was very conscientious in his duties but heavy on the regulator; Dai also worked the last train to Brecon. Driver Reg Bird was a senior driver, a quiet man, but not a good driver, he was very nervous and did not run his trains with confidence.

Another driver, Archie Wikins, used to like to pour cold tea down your neck, he thought that was hilarious; we did not think so. Drivers Glyn and Edgar John were good drivers but Edgar was a quiet man and Glyn liked a laugh and was pleasant to work with.

Driver Charlie Thomas started work as a fireman late in life and was still firing in his fifties. He was eventually made driver and we had to wave to his wife when passing his house in Cadoxton, he used to blow the whistle to her.

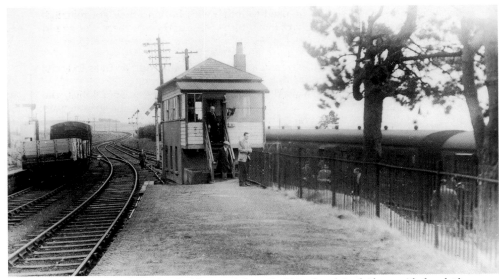

Colbren Junction in 1960 , view looking north from the Ystradgynlais platform with the platform
for Neath trains to the right.   *R.K. Blencowe*

Ex-LMS 0-6-0T 'Jinty' No. 47479 with a special passenger train at the Ystradgynlais platform at
Colbren on 14th July, 1956.   *R.W. Rush*

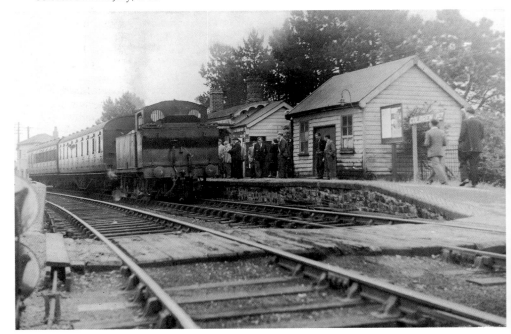

She was 20 years his senior, he used to lodge with her and they got married. One day before I knew this, Charlie was in the cabin and I said there was an old wrinkly waving to us at Cadoxton. Charlie was not happy with this remark saying that was his missus; I had put my foot right in it.

Another driver, Viv Thomas from Cadoxton, also took firemen in as lodgers, he used to do this on a regular basis; Viv was a good driver.

The N&B shed was supervised on a three-shift pattern. Stan Jones, the shedmaster, used to work the 7.00 am to 3.00 pm shift, the shed chargemen used to work 3.00 pm to 11.00 pm and a night shift chargeman 11.00 pm to 7.00 am.

Top Link Drivers
F. Lewis, A. Bracy, A. Davies, D. Hopkins, A. Wilkins, B. Mathias, H. Box, J. James, P. Harvey, J. Edwards (ASLEF Union Rep.)
No. 2 Link
G. John, E. John, C. Thomas, R. Bird, H. Headon, J. Rossman, J. Edwards, B. Scaplehorn, E. Kival and B. Morgan
Pilot Link
D. Powis, G. White, C. Prior, J. Griffiths, L. Powell

In 1963 the depot had two '42XX' class 2-8-0Ts on trial and these were reasonably effective, we also had a '72XX' class 2-8-2T but it became derailed at Seven Sisters Colliery and was moved away. These engines replaced the panniers on the branch and the two locomotives were sufficient to cover the remaining work after some collieries had cut back on supplies or closed altogether.

There were still two or three panniers left and one was for the Resolven tripper, locally known as the 'Jazz' and by that time we had an '08' diesel shunter on the N&B Yard Pilot, the Neath Jn Pilot was withdrawn when the yard closed in early 1964.

When working trains down the branch in 1963 we would run the coal direct to Swansea Docks and return with empties. The Glyn Neath men (Vale of Neath line) also worked their traffic to Swansea Docks from Glyn Neath and returned with empties. It was about this time that the Neath Jn to Neath General bridge closed and all the Vale traffic went through the Low Level station to Swansea Docks or Jersey Marine. Eventually Glyn Neath shed closed and the men were transferred to the N&B shed with their engines.

The LDC (Local Departmental Committee) man at the N&B shed was Jim Jones, he was an excellent union man and met with management on all issues relating to railway work at the shed. He was a top link fireman and his mate was John James who was a real character.

Steam at the N&B went in 1964 and finally the depot closed in 1969. I went to Swansea East Dock as a secondman mostly on class '37' diesels until 1983 when the depot closed. At Swansea I used to pilot the Eastern Depot men, who were now working the branch, from Swansea Docks to Onllwyn with pools and return with coal. I eventually moved to Margam as a secondman working on 'Hymeks', 'Westerns' and class '37s'. I eventually passed on these and after learning the road from Fishguard to Gloucester and Severn Tunnel Jn, I progressed to the driver's position.

Resolven permanent way gang change fish plates and rail chairs in 1949. In the background a wagon is being loaded with small mine coal.   *M. Williams*

Station master Mr Jones with station staff and permanent way gang outside Resolven West signal box in 1949.   *M. Williams*

Guard Gwyn Davies stands next to 0-6-0PT No. 7767 on the 'Jazz' pilot duty at Resolven in 1949.
M. Williams

'72XX' class 2-8-2T No. 7204 runs past Resolven with a through freight.   *Robert Thomas*

'56XX' class 0-6-2T No. 6673 arrives at Resolven with a Pontypool Road-Neath train.
Robert Thomas

350 hp diesel-electric 0-6-0 shunter (later classified '08') No. D3745 on Neath N&B yard pilot duty with driver Bill Scaplehorn and secondman Jim Jones. *W. Scaplehorn*

Staff pose next to English Electric Co-Co type '3' (later class '37') No. D6926 at Neath N&B shed. Bill Scaplehorn is second left and far right is C. Thomas. *W. Scaplehorn*

Glyn Neath engine shed in 1947. Originally built in 1879 the shed had been extended in 1937.
Real Photographs

'94XX' class 0-6-0PT on banking duties outside Glyn Neath shed. The concrete structure over the railway is a bridge to the colliery tip. *Robert Thomas*

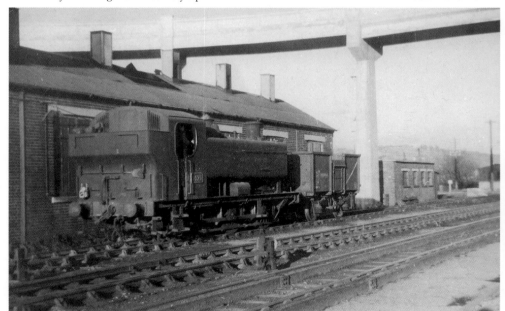

Glyn Neath Sub-shed of 87A

Shed Staff
3 Fire Droppers
1 Shed Labourer
1 Chargeman
3 Cleaners

Drivers/Firemen
10 Sets
1 Spare Set

Shed Duties
1 Pilot and banking turn (3 shifts)
1 Pilot turn - Colliery shunting duties (2 shifts)

Train Duties
9.30 am Glyn Neath to Middle Duffryn (Phurnacite Plant)
2.15 pm Swansea Docks
8.15 pm Control, Swansea Dock/Port Talbot Docks
11.30 pm Control, Swansea Dock/Port Talbot Docks

Some of our duties included steel trains from Margam, stone traffic from Gloucester to Margam, trains to and from Ebbw Vale, trains to Shrewsbury, to Bristol with the Exeter goods, to Reading, working over the Berks & Hants, also working via Stroud over the Golden Grove. I can also remember my first trip through the Tunnel (Black Hole) with its two blue lights at the bottom.

There were approximately 112 drivers at Margam including the sub-depot at Port Talbot, the roster clerk was Harry Miles. Port Talbot was the first diesel depot to have its secondmen taken away in 1989, it became a driver-only depot. Eventually all the work at Port Talbot was transferred to Margam. At Margam I was elected onto the LDC to represent the men, I also became a member of the MAS (Mutual Assurance Society) and became its Margam Vice President. We used to meet with other depots around the country on issues concerning railwaymen's welfare, it was finally wound up on its 100 years anniversary.

Fatalities

I was a secondman on a gas tanker night train which my driver Will Glass and I had taken over at Cardiff on a back working. We were at Baglan Moors when we saw the up sleeper coming towards us at speed. Arriving at Briton Ferry the signal on the main line was at red, I contacted the signalman at Port Talbot who asked if we could examine the train, the up sleeper had reported a bump at Baglan. He said he would signal us into Briton Ferry yard to examine the train. When we got into the yard I got down off the locomotive to look around the train, when I got to the second tank there was evidence of blood and flesh. We did not see anyone but apparently they were crossing the line at Baglan and got caught between the two trains and killed instantly.

Fireman Lyn Baker looks out from the cab of Glyn Neath banker '42XX' class 2-8-0T No. 5242, with chargeman Tom Rees on the locomotive's steps. *Bert Bowen*

Railway staff at Glyn Neath station. *Left to right:* station master Mr Williams and staff Martin and Glan John.   *G. Davies*

Glyn Neath station staff having a tea break. *Left to right*: Glan John, Alex Coole, Martin John, Des Gower.   *A. Price*

A pannier tank with its passenger train crosses Pontwalby viaduct on a local Aberdare-Neath train, with the village of Glyn Neath in the background. Pontwalby Halt is to the right of the viaduct, out of picture, and Rhigos Colliery signal box can be seen to the left of the locomotive.

Author's Collection

'51XX' class 2-6-2T No. 4169 waits for the 'right away' at Glyn Neath on a Pontypool Road-Neath passenger train.   *Robert Thomas*

'51XX' class 2-6-2T No. 4110 is ready with the last steam-hauled goods train to leave Glyn Neath in June 1965. *From left to right are*: Martin Lloyd, driver G. Richards, fireman Lynn Preece, shunter Glan John and guard Alex Coole. Martin Lloyd was not employed by BR, the men clubbed together and gave him a few pounds to look after the cabin fire and make the tea.   *G. Davies*

On another occasion when working back from Cardiff with a down goods, we were pulled up at Ely with a red signal. I went to the phone and the signalman at Cardiff signal box asked me to examine the line because there had been reports of a fatality on the line. I looked forward and could see what looked like a rusty steel coil on the line; I walked to examine this and found it to be a body that had been cut in half. I reported this back to the signalman who asked me if I would remove the body from the line. I shouted to my mate and he said 'no way', and told me to advise the signalman to contact the railway police. I think the signalman was concerned about holding up the passenger trains.

Derailments

In the year 2000 I was driving a steel train to Llanwern. On Bank Holiday Monday afternoon I was put in the loop at Stormy for the passenger and followed him all the way to Cardiff Canton where I received a yellow, it then changed to green for the up relief line. I was proceeding at about 15 mph through the station, I had the road at the end of the station and started to drop down the bank to Newtown when I felt this almighty heave. I dropped my window and looked back and all I could see was a vast cloud of dust. I stopped the train and walked back and when the dust had settled I could see that the train had become derailed, with wagons all over the place. There were seven still attached to the engine and not derailed, the remaining 11 were all derailed, they had ripped up the track, run into a wall, hanging over the bridge. It closed Cardiff station for seven days with massive rail repairs needed.

I was relieved of my duties for a week so I could relax before the inquiry and make out my report. When the inquiry came up it was the most harrowing experience I have ever encountered. There were 16 men on the management table and just me and a union rep. on the other, taking notes. Questions were put to me concerning the derailment and my speed; I was able to put a good case forward as the train had derailed behind the engine and I had no knowledge of the derailment. On the day of the derailment the railway police asked me for a water sample, the medical section came to examine me to see if I was all right; I was off for a further two weeks before starting work, they put me back on the iron ore train to get my confidence back. I then went back to my link duties with an inspector with me to check on my driving.

Two weeks later I was on an Aberthaw train, I had worked from the branch into the works sidings. The signalman had given us the road to proceed, the shunter had climbed up into the cab and we were progressing into the siding over a set of points worked from the signal box when the engine became derailed and turned over on its side with the second locomotive also damaged going into the back of the front engine. The shunter and myself had to climb out onto the top of the stricken engine through the side door and jump down to the ground.

Eventually the railway inspector came, we had to wait for the testing people to come to give a medical and take a water sample. In the inquiry it came out that the signalman had turned the points under the locomotive and he had caused a considerable amount of damage to the track and the two engines.

This was the final straw, being only two weeks after the other derailment, it really shook me up and I was off sick for some time. When I returned to work I had to go to Bristol for a medical and I was advised to take early retirement. I had not got too long left and I had already had 47 years' service on the railway, so I took their advice and took early retirement.

Steam Days Memories (by Danny Counsell)

On 11th March, 1947 a set of Brecon men had worked a goods train from Brecon with two engines to deal with a heavy load and after putting off at Colbren they picked up their return traffic and left Colbren at 2.15 pm for Brecon with a full banker load. By this time it had begun to snow heavily although it had been snowing all day, but at midday it came down very heavily and when the return Brecon goods arrived at the Penwyllt Brick Works they hit a snow block and stopped. The train staff decided to uncouple and ram the snowdrift but failed and got stuck, a third locomotive was brought up to the rear from Colbren and also got stuck, a further two engines were brought in from Brecon to assist but they got stuck on the top of the Blwch. There were now five engines stuck in the drift, all of which had to have their fires dropped to save the boilers. The train and locomotives were there for a couple of days before being released.

On a Saturday in March 1952 our train left Abercrave Colliery with 25 wagons of coal for Ynysgeinon Jn. The first wagon next to the engine was a 16 ton steel wagon and the second wagon was a 10 ton wooden former private owner's wagon. At Penrhos Brick Works on a bad rail joint on a curve, the 10 ton wagon's buffer dropped under the 16 ton wagon's buffer and became derailed, 14 other wagons becoming derailed causing considerable damage. The engine driver was Aubrey Bracy and the locomotive was No. 7707. A second locomotive was sent for which came from the Colbren end and took the remaining coal wagons to Colbren. The railway accident at Penrhos instigated an unusual working. Because the incident was so serious causing 15 wagons to derail and some of the wagons turned on their sides, to enable train working to resume a loop section was put in place to bypass the derailed wagons. This lasted for six weeks until all the wagons were cut up on site and taken away, it was also necessary to move over 100 tons of coal from the accident site. When this was achieved the line was repaired, the temporary loop taken out and trains resumed normal working from Colbren to Ynisgeinon.

There were 12 guards at the N&B all in one link, also there were two passenger guards that only used to work the 8.25 am and 4.10 pm services to Brecon. One turn on the N&B covered by Neath shed in my time was the 5.00 pm goods to Onllwyn and the return, also a Neath guard worked this duty.

Another accident which occurred when I was a guard at the N&B was at Cefn Coed Colliery; it happened at 4.00 am. I had picked up my coal train from the colliery sidings and the engine had pulled out onto the branch and stopped

The derailment at Penrhos in March 1952. The permanent way staff are at work contructing a
temporary bypass loop.   *(Both) L. Morgan*

clear of the points. I reversed the point and was about to climb on the brake van to drop it down onto the train when nine loaded coal wagons came past me from the colliery sidings and ran through the catch points and into the drag and turned over onto the branch metals between the train and the brake van. There was coal everywhere and this accident blocked the branch for hours.

The Glyn Neath men used to work 70 loaded coal wagons from Glyn Neath to Swansea Docks on the understanding that they had a clear road from Glyn Neath to the Docks.

There were two items that were important to train working over the N&B branch in cold weather – the water columns at Crynant and Colbren. The fire devils were kept going on a 24 hour basis; N&B cleaners had to look after them and covered these on a shift pattern. The engines used to drop coal off at these points for the cleaners to man the fire devils.

Port Talbot Railway to Tonmawr

The Port Talbot Railway that ran from Port Talbot (Aberavon station) in the early 1900s used to provide a shopping service for the village of Tonmawr because there were no shops there. The daily train guard took food orders and the villagers used to give the orders to the guard on Tuesdays and these would return by train on Thursdays when the Tonmawr residents picked up their orders and paid the guard. This was arranged with a local shop at Aberavon and a fee was charged for this service

The Port Talbot Railway was opened in 1898 and ran six miles to Tonmawr platform with another two miles of colliery lines, one to Blaenavon Colliery and another to the Whitworth Colliery. Both collieries were closed by 1964.

PENWYLLT

Fatal Accident to Railway Porter - Quite a gloom was cast over Penwyllt when the sad news was received on Wednesday morning, December 21st, that Leonard, the youngest son of Mr and Mrs Bamister, Penypant, who was employed as a porter at Seven Sisters Station had been killed that morning by a passing engine and van. The funeral, which took place on Monday, December 26th was largely attended from a wide area, showing the respect and sympathy felt for the aged father and mother, the former a retired signalman from Craigynos station. The chief mourners were the mother and brothers. The father was ill and unable to leave home and the only sister was stranded *en route* from Leominster at Three Cocks, the fall of snow on Christmas Day having made the roads impassable in many parts. From the house to Callwen Church a large gang of willing helpers turned out and cleared passages through the heavy drifts to enable the coffin to be taken to its resting place. There were floral tributes from the parents, sister and brothers also from many friends, including the staff at Seven Sisters and the staff at Craigynos, where the deceased was previously employed. A large number of railwaymen also attended in uniform. The sympathy of everyone in the district is extended to the parents, as Leonard was a most bright and happy young fellow of 22 years of age. Mr T. Morgan conducted the service at the house and the Rev. D. Hughes at Callwen Church. Mr L. Davies of Penwyllt, made the funeral arrangements.

The aftermath of the derailment at Court Sart Farm occupation crossing on 9th October, 1950.
(Both) Gerald Williams

District Lampman to Yard Inspector (by Jack Jones)

Jack Jones started his railway career in the Ammanford district and worked at Glanamman, Garnant and Gwaun-cae-Gurwen stations. Jack also worked as district lampman for two years. His weekly schedule was a six-day operation and covered 20 miles from Genwen Jn (Bynea) in the South to Derwydd Road on the Central Wales Line in the North.

He used to fill 360 lamps a week, using 20 gallons of paraffin in the process. He would carry two gallon cans and a bottle of meths and rags for cleaning, and a shed full of matches for re-lighting. When the cans became empty or low he would top them up at lamp huts at stations or signal boxes he passed on the way. Also part of his duty was to keep the lamp hut paraffin containers full to enable him to carry out his duties. His meal breaks were at stations or signal boxes on the way.

The job was extremely difficult in bad weather, heavy rain would cause problems with water in the paraffin and inevitably would lead to some lamps going out. This resulted in reports from train crews unable to see signals in the dark, culminating in Jack being called out to rectify the problems.

Another problem was high winds, some of the signals were very high and used to sway in high winds; there were no safety harnesses in the old days so you had to hang on. The lamps wells took seven days to empty and it was important to keep up the six-day operation.

Jack was glad to see the back of this job when he applied for a goods guard position at Swansea East Dock and got it, he later moved on as foreman at Llandilo Jn, Llanelli and finished up as yard inspector at Margam Sorting Sidings.

Jack Jones recalls that a Swansea Eastern Depot train was returning from Aberdare when the driver failed to hold his train on the Glyn Neath bank and ran into the sand drag at Pontwalby knocking the guard out and causing him minor injuries. The guard was taken to Swansea Hospital for treatment. While he was there the Luftwaffe dropped a bomb on the hospital and knocked him out a second time, but he recovered and took up his railway duties again at Swansea East Dock!

On 9th October, 1950 Jack was travelling 'on the cushions' in the second carriage on the 2.10 pm service from Cardiff to Swansea when the train struck a Scammell lorry at Court Sart Farm occupation crossing and the engine and carriages became derailed. He was thrown about and shaken up but was otherwise uninjured. Jack took prompt action in running up the line assisting in the placing of detonaters to protect the train from the oncoming passenger train from Neath. He received a commendation for his actions from the operating superintendent. There was also a commendation for signalman Geoffrey Evans at Neath Engine Shed signal box who promptly placed the signal at danger.

Another tale that Jack portrayed was when working the 3.15 am Cardiff with a train of bogie bolsters, this type of vehicle always being conveyed on this train. When he contacted control they advised him that his train was at Burrows Sidings. So they left Eastern Depot, engine and van, for the Burrows and joined the train. Jack walked around the train and noticed all the chains were hanging

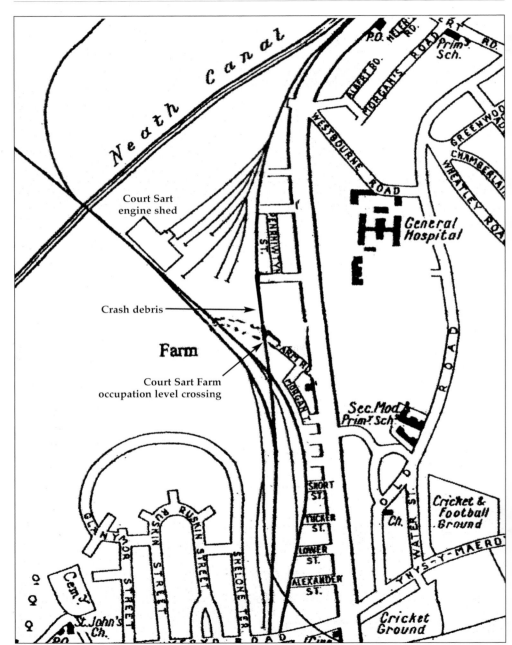

A map adapted from the accident report which shows the site of the incident at Neath Court Sart Farm occupation level crossing on 9th October, 1950.

The derailment at Court Sart Farm occupation crossing attracted a good number of onlookers.
Gerald Williams

The train engine, a '51XX' class 2-6-2T is lifted by a pair of breakdown cranes. *Gerald Williams*

Briton Ferry yard shunters and foreman Percy King (*far right*) taking a break for the photographer. Percy King (the author's father) moved from guard at Swansea Eastern Depot to foreman in line of promotion.   *Author*

Shunters and staff at Margam. Jack Jones is second from the right in the second row.

Jack Jones

down making the bolsters unsafe to travel, so he went back on the phone to control and advised them of the problem. After a few choice words he was advised to run engine and van to Jersey Marine and pick up a train of bolsters from there. Off they went to Jersey and backed on the train, again Jack walked around the train only to notice that here also all the chains were hanging down, making the traffic unsafe. Once more he phoned the control advising them of the unsafe condition of the traffic. By this time the controller was quite aerated and again vented his vocabulary on Jack and told him to '****** off home', so it was back to the depot, engine and van, and an early finish for the boys!

Some of the staff at Swansea Eastern Depot that Jack can remember

Shed Staff (1959)
Office: Reg Wintle (shedmaster)
Clerks: Dick Parsons, Hilton Lloyd, Brian Davies (relief), Ken Phillips (relief)
Shed Staff: Richie Butler (fire lighter), Tom Fox (stores), Trevor Burtonshaw and George Phillips (shed foremen), Alfie Pipes (foreman fitter), George Riley and Charlie Benjamin (shed prepmen)

Drivers
No. 1 Link Drivers: Frank Bowen, Bill Rees
Train Links: Badyn Powell, Hector Mack, Stan Mitchell, Tommy Simson, Geoff Reed, Frank Wheeler, Joe Davey, Cliff Smith

Shunting Pilot Drivers
Tom Cook, Jack Bebell, Percy Lloyd, Archie Rue

Firemen
Peter Hutchinson, Don King, Gordon Perry, Brian Neiman, Len Humphries, Fred Bebell, Arthur Hutchinson, Roy Hutchinson, Frank King

Guards
Percy King, Jack Jones, Dai Rate, Jack Goodfellow, Roy Polson, Dai Jones, Billy Morris, Les Thomas, Reg Beynon, Ken Hendy, Bert Jarvis, Albert Chambers, Bill Rees, Danny Evans, Trevor Francis, George Pittard, Evan Williams, Jack Davies, Fred Stone, George Thomas, Colin Sterns, Bill Brown, Les Rees, Jack Cadwallader, Ivor Cadwallader, Ben Hughes, Trevor Hughes, Billy Costello, Ray Davies, Ivor Tucker

More drivers/firemen
Frank Bowen (jnr), Toddy Fritsgerald, Ted Williams, Elvert Walters, Walter Jones, Charlie Cotterell, Charlie Brooks, Bill Harding, Jackie Robinson, Billy Rowlands, Gordon Percy, Humphrey Williams, Len Miller, Cliff Williams, George Young, Bill Everson, Bill Lewis, Danny Hoskins, Bill Davies, Alan Phelps, George Heathaway.

Faggot Boy to HST Driver (by Howard Jones)

I started with British Railways on 14th January, 1952 as a faggot boy in the carriage shops making fire lighters. A month later I was transferred to the main shed as a cleaner under the supervision of Messrs Cook, Arthur Miller and Arthur Dyer. My first firing turn came later in the year with Fred Fisher on the

Margam yard under construction in July 1959. The yard was opened in April 1960 and consisted of 33 miles of track and 240 points. *Great Western Trust*

'42XX' class 2-8-0T No. 5225 battles up Stormy bank on 14th March, 1962 with an eastbound freight train. A pannier tank gives assistance at the rear. *R.O. Tuck/Rail Archive Stephenson*

station pilot starting at midday. More turns became available as men were leaving with the Margam Steelworks being constructed.

In 1953 I was made a fireman for Neath & Brecon. Regular journeys were to Brecon, Colbren, Onllwyn on the coal trains which were working in the valley at that time. I was later promoted to Dyffryn Yard working on the 'bankers' and the trains through to Maesteg, Pontycymmer, Neath Road. The line was becoming redundant in this area though. I worked on the Docks pilot and all the pilots in Margam at that time. This was a particularly enjoyable time to be working for British Railways.

At the end of 1954 I joined the army for National Service leaving in 1957 and returning to Neath as a fireman. I was working all the valleys including destinations such as Pontypool, Aberdare, Abercynon, Porthcawl and Treherbert. All this work was on steam trains. 1958 saw the introduction of diesels. More frequent steam turns in Neath became available going from Neath shed to Landore, Swansea (High Street) over to Felin Fran and working the milk trains to Cardiff.

Soon steam began to be phased out. I worked the inspection coach from Neath to Hirwaun, down the Penderyn branch, over to Merthyr then up to Brecon and returning over the branch line to Colbren, Onllwyn and back to Neath, finally returning to Neath yard putting the coach off and the engine to shed.

The Neath and Brecon branch closed to passengers with some of the remaining work being done from Neath and some from Eastern Depot. The Glyn Neath depot also closed at this time. Aberdare closed with no further bank work trains stopping at Cwmgwrach.

Steam trains were still running upon the closure of the Neath branch in March 1965. I then moved to Neath station and finally saw the end of the steam era.

One of my last jobs on a steam train was taking class '9F' 2-10-0 No. 92220 *Evening Star* from Neath to Severn Tunnel Junction leaving it on the pit and I remember months later taking diesel trains to Gloucester. The *Evening Star* was still there just rusting away before it was finally rescued for a Museum with enthusiasts refurbishing it for some limited main line use. (It is currently at Swindon STEAM Museum.)

There was some interesting work on diesels working up to Garw, Ogwr Valley and over to Waun Tarw. After the crash at Bridgend in 1967 trains then went over Waun Tarw coming out at Llanharan or going to Aberdare then via Hengoed and Risca before the line was repaired. Shortly after reopening the main line, the Waun Tarw line was closed.

From 1967 work from Margam was limited to the Garw and Ogwr Valley but then came the introduction of oil trains to Gloucester. Trains to Tungsted were also introduced and after working at Margam for some years I was finally promoted to driver.

My first preference was Swansea (High Street) though and eventually I was promoted to that station. I then started driving the High Speed Trains (HST) and the diesel-multiple-units (dmus) and all the traction in Swansea doing all the branch work including Fishguard, Pembroke and the Central Wales line. Years before I had worked steam trains into Neyland and Fishguard and the diesels certainly made the work a lot easier.

BRITISH RAILWAYS (W.R.)   **PASSENGER TRAIN JOURNAL.**   B.R. 29752/2

(For full instructions in making out this Journal see Circular No. 4820 dated January 1935)

DOWN

Passenger { Description of Train } 10 __ m. from _Paddington_ to _____

Shew here the Ordinary Train of which the above is a Train run in relief thereof } 15 m. from _Paddington_ to _Swansea_ HL

Monday, 26 March 1979   1. C 32

Stations and Dividing Points between each District	ACTUAL TIME OF		Late away from Station Mins.	MINUTES LOST						MINUTES GAINED		VEHICLES				Tare-weight in Tons at starting point and where load is altered	Remarks as to cause of detentions at Stations, Signals, etc., also information shewing the various places where Train is crossed from M.L. to R.L. or vice versa
	Arrival	Departure		At Stations			By Engine	By Signals	By Eng. Checks	By Exceptional Causes	At Station	By Engine	Attached		Detached			
	H. M.	H. M.	H. M.	Attaching or Detaching	Other Station delays	Waiting Connections							Loaded	Empty	Loaded	Empty		
Paddington		10 15	—										9				382	
Reading	10 37	10 39	—			2												R.O.S.
Neath Jcn		11 12	2					8½										Working Neath Train of detaching passengers stock on off track
Bristol P.W.	11 31	11 39	10															
Pur... P.W.		11 38	10½					6	2									R.O.S. Train held at sig. off East
Newport	12 05	12 07	18½									3						R.O.S.
Cardiff	12 22	12 25	18½															R.O.S.
Bridgend	12 48½	12 55	17½					½			1							
Port Talbot	12 53	12 59	19½					3				2						Broken Rail nr Talbot
Neath	13 05	13 07	17½															R.O.S.
Swansea	13 23		19										9					
TOTALS			19		16	7½						3						

Minutes Late *both* Districts or at Destination   19

Total of all Minutes in District
Lost   22   Gained   3

State of Weather during Journey, if Wet, Frost, Fog or Snow, and between what Points   *Heavy Rain*

General Remarks, e.g., Occurrences to Train, Causes of Delay, whether Coaches fully and correctly labelled, properly heated and suggestions for improvement of Working, etc.

Shew "Yes" or "No" if Train is formed in accordance with programme, etc.

NUMBER OF PASSENGERS IN TRAIN ON LEAVING									Shew "Yes" or "No" if Train is clean and in good condition; if not give particulars and Coach Numbers.
Paddington		Reading		Bristol P.W.		Cardiff		Neath		
First	Second	First	Second	First	Second	First	Second	First	Second
19	121	21	176	23	141	6	108	1	118

On 3rd November, 1975 the HST made its first passenger run into South Wales with a daily return trip to Swansea leaving Paddington at 9.00 am and departing from Swansea for the return journey at 12.52. It was not until 4th October, 1976 that a complete service of 11 trains each way daily was operated between Paddington and Swansea. This is the passenger train journal for an HST trip on 26th March, 1979.

Following privatisation the work was not so interesting, losing much of the Valleys work but starting to go to London. I had a nasty experience when working the 6.00 am HST from Swansea to Paddington. At Reading I had a signal check and was put onto the relief line due to engineering work, I eventually regained the main line and picked up speed to make up lost time. When running through Action station at speed I suddenly saw workmen on lightweight scaffolding under a bridge at the end of the platform; I put in an emergency brake application but ploughed into the scaffolding with the men working on it; the train eventually stopping some way past the incident. I dropped down from the cab to go to the phone and contacted the signalman and asked him why he had allowed P-Way men to work on the main line when I had a green to go through the station. He was taken back by this and advised me that the men involved should not be working in this area and he would look into why they were there. I walked back to see the men and thankfully they were not seriously injured but found out that they were working in the wrong area and should not have been there. I was eventually allowed to continue after the safety officer had taken notes and the men had been attended to. I arrived at Paddington somewhat shaken and later than intended.

I worked the Swansea to Paddington route for a number of years until unfortunately I passed a red light and tendered my resignation on 6th December, 1996, just a couple of weeks short of the day 45 years earlier when I started as a faggot boy in the carriage shops.

A contrast in main line motive power. Preserved GWR 'King' class 4-6-0 No. *King George V* bears the 'Capitals United Express' headboard at Swansea (High Street) station in September 1987. This was the first time a 'King' class locomotive had been seen in Swansea, as, in steam days, these engines were not permitted west of Cardiff. Alongside was the contemporary motive power for South Wales expresses, an HST set.   *Author*

Margam duties 1968/9 (diesel turns)
Taken from guard's book of Roy Stephens, Margam

01.20	Margam to Velindre
02.20	Albion to Waterston (work from Hereford)
03.35	Margam to Northwich
05.25	Margam to Cardiff Tidal Sidings
05.30	Margam to Severn Tunnel Jn
05.50	Llandarcy to Ebbw Vale (Duffryn Sds)
05.55	Margam to Herbrandston
06.00	Briton Ferry to Landore Goods
06.00	Carlisle to Herbrandston
07.20	Margam to Radyr
08.00	Danygraig to Barry
08.50	Margam to Fishguard
08.50	Margam to Pembrey
08.55	Winsford to Neath (Court Sart)
09.15	Margam to Velindre
09.49	Ebbw Vale Duffryn Sidings to Llandarcy
09.50	Cardiff Tidal Sidings to Margam
09.50	Margam to Llanwern
09.50	Llanwern to Margam
09.51	Margam to Trostre
10.30	Hereford to Margam
11.40	Llandarcy to Avonmouth
12.00	Margam to Barry
12.00	Rowley Regis to Llandarcy (relieve Gloucester 14.03)
12.35	Llandarcy to Llanwern
12.50	Herbrandston to Proven
12.55	Margam to Hereford (Barrs Court)
13.00	Llandarcy to Rowley Regis (relief at Gloucester)
13.50	Margam to Llanwern
14.00	Margam to Pembrey
14.05	Severn Tunnel to Margam
14.45	Briton Ferry, Metal Box, Briton Ferry
14.58	Jersey Marine to Severn Tunnel Jn
16.10	Middlewich to Briton Ferry
16.20	Danygraig to Sheffield
17.10	Garston to Danygraig
17.55	Trostre to Llanwern
18.05	Llanwern to Margam
18.15	Reading to Jersey Marine (relieve Severn Tunnel Jn)
18.30	Swansea High Street to Paddington (relief Margam Moors)
19.05	Cardiff (Long Dyke) to Margam
19.40	Nottingham to Swansea High Street
20.20	Burrows Sidings to Dagenham
20.50	Severn Tunnel to Briton Ferry
21.25	Paddington to Swansea
22.08	Dagenham to Swansea Docks
22.28	Briton Ferry to Wolverhampton
22.30	Margam to Hereford (Barrs Court)
22.40	Llanwern to Margam
23.08	Carlisle to Llandarcy
23.20	Margam to Swindon. Pick up slabs Llanwern, relief at Severn Tunnel Jn
23.25	Margam to Bridgend and return

I thoroughly enjoyed my time with the railway but I feel I have seen the best of it. Today I feel the rail network is driven by profit only with no other consideration, but that is no longer my concern and I am now happy to enjoy my retirement.

By 1968 all footplate staff who were working in the Neath area also Swansea East Dock, Danygraig and Duffryn Yard all moved to Margam Diesel Depot, shown opposite are some of the turns they would have worked at that time.

Duffryn Yard shed closed in March 1964 and the men moved directly to the new shed at Margam, also the Tondu shed closed in 1964, the staff also moving to Margam. After the closure of Neath shed in 1965 the loco staff moved to Neath Yard where they stabled the diesels, they eventually moved to Margam in 1967.

The Swansea Eastern Depot shed closed to steam in 1964 but remained open for diesel locomotives for some time until the shed closed and the locomotives were stabled in Eastern Depot Yard until 1983. They then went to Margam and joined the combination of men from Duffryn Yard, Tondu, Neath, Danygraig and Swansea Eastern Depot; Danygraig men had moved to Swansea Eastern Depot in 1960.

Railway Wives (by Pat King)

My grandfather was station master at the Midland station in St Thomas (Swansea), my two uncles, one a signalman at St Thomas, the other a ganger working in the Swansea area. My Dad was the odd one out, working as a wagon repairer at the Road & Rail Company at Upper Bank Works.

In 1950 I can vividly remember Bryan's terraced house at No. 23, Maesteg Street, Kilvey, Swansea, which his father had purchased. The house had three downstairs rooms, the best room in the front, 'The Parlour', was set up with the best furniture and a wind-up gramophone for playing records also a piano which nobody played; there was a coal firegrate with a tiled surround.

The living room, 'Middle room' saw a large fireplace with cast-iron swinging hobs, a side cast-iron oven and a polished copper fender and fireguards. The mantelpiece was high and wooden and painted in dark brown, there was a large farmhouse table in the middle of the room covered with a thick table cloth, with farmhouse chairs to match. There was a valve type wireless on the kitchen cabinet and two fireside chairs in the room.

Moving to the back kitchen there was another old type fireplace similar to the one in the middle room, there was a Belfast sink and cold water tap by the window with a wooden draining board fixed to the side of the sink. There was a washing board hanging on the wall and a small table and two chairs against the wall, also a door leading to a pantry under the stairs with large hooks in the ceiling section and a large stone slab at the back of the pantry.

Outside the back door there was a small glass lean-to in which hung a large tin bath and two tin buckets for filling the bath, these were put on the fire hobs to warm the water for bath nights.

Upstairs saw three bedrooms, two reasonably sized and one very small, just enough room for a single bed and a chair.

A typical railwayman's cottage in the early 1950s.   *Author's Collection*

In the garden was an outside toilet, a coal shed and at the bottom of the garden a World War II air raid shelter. The shelter had three bunk beds to one side and a row of chairs on the other side, with a small table at the far end, I can remember spending many a night in the shelter when the Germans were bombing Swansea.

This was a typical railwayman's terraced house of the 1940s/50s and was duplicated all over the country. These did not change until the 1960s when televisions went into production and part of the back kitchen was altered to accommodate a bath; what luxury.

My role as a railwayman's wife began in 1960, both our families have various railway connections. Bryan's dad was a guard, his brother a fireman and of course Bryan, a young fireman at the time, all working from the Swansea East Dock shed.

I can remember Bryan's mum saying how she used to get up at all hours in the night to cook, make tea, plus made their food boxes before they would go off to work. She also described washing day which would always be on Monday mornings, she would soak all their overall trousers and coats in a large tin bath which would be kept outside the back door, on Sunday nights. Then, first thing on Monday, down from the peg in the shed, the scrubbing board would be used to scrub the oil and grime from the men's overalls; it was hard work.

By the time I became a railwayman's wife the first washing machine became available, complete with wringer attached, rented then bought. Wasn't I the lucky one to acquire this wonderful invention?

When Bryan and I were first married I was surprised at the time he spent in work, he would go off in the morning and would not return until late at night.

This was on a regular basis, so the only time we got to see each other properly was at weekends.

When Bryan left the footplate and went to work in Margam as a carriage & wagon examiner, our life became much easier, with regular shift patterns, but when he transferred to a guard's position at Margam the old patterns of train work emerged and he was back to long shifts again. So you will understand that railway work, especially on the trains was very unpredictable. There were no set timings and a railwayman's wife's work was unsettling, he was either in work or in bed. To be honest I was glad when he left the railway so I could run a normal family life.

David John Morgan (by Adrian Jones)

My grandfather was David John Morgan, otherwise known as 'Dai'. He was born in 1887 and was sent at 10 to Narberth to his grandparents to be apprenticed as a wheelwright. This did not work out and he came back home to the family at Rosser Street in Neath. He then went on to work in a colliery (drift mine) near the Ivy Tower, but gave this up when he was pulled out following a roof-fall. I am not sure of his next move, but he turned up at the Neath & Brecon as a cleaner, going up through fireman to driver. I suppose he must have started about 1902-4 and eventually retired in the winter of 1947/48.

I think he must have been a bit of a thorn in the flesh of the Neath & Brecon Co. in independent days since he was on the ASLEF committee, and I well recall him recounting how he threatened to pull the men out over a halfpenny - an - hour rise. I do have a medal given to him for proposing 26 new members in the Neath Branch in 1917/18. I also know that he was active in the local Labour Party circles as he would swap turns for whole weeks to go canvassing and was one of the workers involved in getting Ramsay McDonald elected. I think he was also involved in the Mutual Improvement classes. I never did understand why he stayed at Riverside all his working life, but it must have somehow suited.

One of the favourite tales was of rescuing a goods train somewhere upline of Colbren. It used to sound so dramatic. I have absolutely no idea of the year, but it was a bitterly cold winter and snow had been blowing thickly... an LMS goods train had run up from Swansea with a tender engine at the front and a tank engine banking. This stuck in a drift right up in the mountains. For some reason Riverside engine and crews were turned out to rescue this. (He never said why ... was the line down to Ynysgeinon blocked, or did Upper Bank have nothing in steam?) Anyway three engines were turned out and eventually reached the scene, and after a great struggle managed to drag the train back out. By all accounts the train engine driver was suffering from hypothermia since the cab was an open one. The line remained blocked for several days and when trains did get through again, the carriage ventilators were showing the depth of the snow where it had rubbed.

Grampa must have worked on the passenger turns quite a lot as he knew the regular travellers very well. There was a group of women lodging in Neath who

N&B passenger trains would reach journey's end at Brecon (Free Street) station having travelled a little over 33 miles. This view of the Colbren Junction (western) end of the platforms at Brecon dates from around 1910.   *Lens of Sutton Collection*

Seven Sisters colliery and station looking towards Brecon.   *Author's Collection*

taught up the valley at Crynant and Seven Sisters, travelling up on the morning train. One of them, Miss Gertie Bowen of Cadoxton, used often to recount how he would watch them crossing the bridge at Riverside and then blow the whistle to make them think he was about to start. However, if a message had come that one of them was delayed, he was known to look the other way when the guard was waving the flag, until the errant traveller arrived.

It's strange how there are people around these days who don't believe that breakfast was cooked on the shovel. Of course it was after a dousing of boiling water. I understand also that tea was taken in a can without the milk which was brought in a separate glass bottle to prevent curdling when the can was above the firebox door. Another odd fact about N&B yard was that crews on shunting turns used to swim in the canal and then dry off by their fires.

The last train up on Saturday night was an institution. The communication cord was always pulled to effect a convenient stopping place for isolated farms and cottages, whereupon a pair of legs would have been seen disappearing across a field. Frequently as the train got under way again one of the seat cushions would be thrown out, to be collected later and used on the settle by some farm fireplace.

Sheep were something of a hazard up line. Clearance was attempted by blowing steam if you were going forwards or pelting lumps of coal if you were bunker first.

He did also mention the colliers' trains. It was always the case that as the bunker of the engine emerged from the bridge under the GW main line, every door would be open, and, before the engine had stopped, the first runners would be at the top of the stairs. Anyone foolish enough to be on Bridge Street (Neath) at the time was advised to hide in shop doorways to avoid a blackening.

Railwaymen at Colbren Junction in 1931. Far left is fireman Viv Thomas and driver David Morgan is second from right.   *Adrian Jones*

Glossary of Footplate Terms

Ashpan Dampers	Levers that connect to doors, front and rear of ashpan below the fire grate to allow air through the fire bars to burn the coal.
ATC	A safety device (Automatic Train Control) on the footplate indicating when distant signals are at caution or clear. If the driver does not react to a caution signal the brakes will automatically be applied.
Bag (railway slang term)	Flexible pipe on water column.
Bar or Dart	Long bar for clearing the fire bars of clinker.
Blast Pipe (Jumper)	A pipe in smoke box with blower 'jumper' steam-operated device on top of the blast pipe, it helps to excite the fire and prevents blow backs from fire into cab.
Blowing off	Excess steam being released by the safety valve.
'Board' (railway slang term)	Signal.
'Bobby' (railway slang term)	Signalman (in early days known as policemen).
Brick Arch	An arch of fire bricks fitted in the roof of the firebox in front of the tubeplate, protects tubes from direct flames, it also assists gases in the firebox.
'Caped' (telegraphic code)	Train cancelled.
Cocks	Cocks fitted to cylinders that drain water from cylinders.
Exhaust Injectors	Utilising exhaust steam (waste steam) they provide a supply of hot feed water to boiler, and are not so severe as the cold water injector on the boiler and would not react as severely on the steam pressure as would a cold feed injector. They would only operate when the regulator was open, and if the regulator was closed the injector would automatically change to cold water feed. These injectors would normally be found on the passenger type engines.
Flap	Firehole flap fixed by chain to main firehole door handle, used by fireman in preference to main sliding doors, allows more air to flow through fire.
Gauge Glass	A device in the cab which shows the amount of water in the boiler.
'Got the road'	This is a railway term for the signal being lowered allowing the passage of the train into the next section of line.
Injector	A valve fitted on footplate (front of cab) to supply steam and water into boiler, cold water lever fitted on tender or on bunker section (in cab) of tank engines.
Pep Pipe (or Slack Pipe)	A pipe fitted to a controlled valve for washing down footplate and watering coal.
Pools	Empty wagons (usually coal empties).
Pricker	Long bar with an end bent at 90º for lifting the fire.

Appendix Two

Locomotive Driver's Contract, May 1858

This item will be of particular interest to locomen and others who worked in the era of steam. It is reproduced from the Newport Maesglas Area News, No. 15 by kind permission of Area Manager, Stan Tindall.

I, the undersigned, do hereby undertake for and in consideration of the sum of five pence per train mile run to be paid to me by the London & North Western Railway company, to drive an engine working goods trains between Rugby and Northampton, or elsewhere and to provide and pay all wages to my Fireman and Cleaner and to provide the necessary firewood, coke, coal, oil, tallow, tender hose pipes, gauge glasses, tender brake blocks, cotton waste flax for packing and all small stores of every kind which may be required.

Also to repair or pay the cost of repairs to all the following parts: Piston packing slide valves, glands, connecting rod brasses, pumps and valves, to maintain my stock of tools, and to pay for putting in pistons and valve springs, lining up all brasses, rods or slide bars, letting together all brasses or straps, making steam and all other joints, and putting all the necessary pins, bushes and bolts in the working parts.

I also engage to do or tender full assistance as far as possible towards whatever may be required to be done to my engine and tender on shed days, or at other times and to do whatever else may be required to keep the engine in perfect working order so long as it is under my charge, with the exception of providing such articles as are of iron, brass, copper or steel, or of paying for other labour that may be necessary to be done at Wolverton, or otherwise in cases of accident resulting from causes beyond my control.

And I undertake to abide by and attend strictly to all the rules of the company and to use all the means in my power to ensure the punctual arrival of my trains at all stations, and in case I require assistance I agree to be charged at the rate of five pence per mile, for every mile assisted, and provided I am required to pilot or assist another train or engine, I agree to accept payment for such work at the rate of five pence per mile for the miles assisted and half-price for empty miles.

And I further agree, in the event of losing time in the working of my train without being able to show sufficient cause, or of not using due exertion to keep my time, to subject myself to any reasonable fine that my superintendent may inflict, and in case my engine should fail on the road from defective pumps, or any other cause arising from my neglect and another engine should be required to take the train forward, I will subject myself to any reasonable charge my superintendent may determine.

And I do further agree that in case of breakage to any part of my engine, or damage to any stock, caused by my neglect, I will submit to pay the cost of repairs, or such sum as my superintendent may direct.

And lastly, in case I or my superintendent desire to alter the terms of, or otherwise terminate, this contract, I agree to give or to accept from him a fortnight's notice in writing, and, in case of difference, I agree that an appeal to the directors shall be final and conclusive.

The prices to be charged for stores include coke 24s. a ton, coal 12s. 6d. a ton, oil 5d. a pint, tallow 6d. a pound, yellow grease 2d. a pound, cotton waste 2d. a pound, and firewood 5d. per cwt.

From the Viv Guerrier Collection

Appendix Three

Shed Duties

Loco Running Shed Foreman
Chareghand Cleaner, Cleaners

It is from engine cleaners that the firemen are invariably appointed. Youths join at the ages between 16 and 21 years, with the very meritorious ambition of eventually becoming drivers, the rigorous sight and stature tests, with other examinations, however, throw many out. The cleaning is performed in gangs, and each is responsible for its allotted number of engines per day or per night as the case may be.

'Not to be moved' boards should be conspicuously exhibited at the back and front of each engine being cleaned as a precaution against its being moved. Similar boards are also used when any fitter or other workman is underneath.

Young men of approved physique and character are promoted from cleaning to act as firemen, in which capacity they fill casual vacancies and also provide the necessary relief at stations where the ordinary men take rest. The spare fireman received a permanent appointment in time, and eventually qualifies for driver, commencing his duties in this capacity as a spare or shed driver.

One other class of employee should be mentioned, viz. the call-boys or messengers, whose duty it is to warn drivers of their booked times at all hours of the night; they also act as general messengers for the office. From call-boy to cleaner, from cleaner to fireman, and from fireman to driver represents the three stages many occupants of the footplate have passed through in their long and honourable career in the railway service.

The following may be taken as a specimen of the report which should be sent to headquarters by a running-shed foreman on the occasion of a locomotive going into the shops for general repairs.

Required to Engine No. - - - - - Boiler, outside to be examined; bad leakage of steam from beneath lagging-plates, all wash-out plug-holes to be re-tapped and mud-hole joints renewed; badly grooved; inside to be examined, all incrustations to be cleared out.

Fire-box to be examined; bottom portion of fire-box sides reduced in thickness, tube-plate cracked in both top corners, fire-hole ring leaking, rivet heads so much reduced as to require renewing, front corners of foundation ring leaking, renew rivets, roof bolts to be renewed and top of fire-box cleared of incrustation.

Stays to be examined: bottom rows to be renewed, heads badly reduced, slight bulging of plate at lower portion of left side; brick-arch studs to be renewed.

Tubes to be examined: new tubes required, tube-plate fractured at both top corners; throat palm stays require renewing, heads being reduced.

Smoke-box to be examined: side plates very thin, drawing air; new door required, being bulged at bottom and drawing air; new chimney wanted; engine steaming badly.

Ash-pan to be examined; side plates thin, both dampers require renewal and gear to be overhauled.

Coalmen

Specially appointed labourers are the coalmen employed in stacking the coal as it comes in, and also for loading on to the engines. The work is usually paid for by contract at a fixed rate per ton. After a stack has been built to the specified dimensions it is customary to whitewash it all round, or at least the corners, so that any disturbance of its bulk can be readily detected.

One man will stack 20 tons of coal per day, inclusive of 'walling.' Piecework prices range from 7*d*. to 9*d*. per ton, according to the locality. Bituminous coal used for stacking may usually be taken to run out at 45 lb. per cub. ft. of stack, and Welsh coal at 55 lb. per cub. ft. A section of an average coal-stack 1 ft square at the base and 9 ft high will equal approximately one-fifth ton.

Store Chargehand
Storekeepers

Neath Stores

The stores are in charge by [*sic*] a head storekeeper, who keeps account of all receipts and issues; he is responsible for the correct issue of lubricating oil, waste, etc., according to the specified allowance per engine for, say, a 100 miles' run. There are usually at least three grades of oil stored for general use; engine or lubricating oil for the axle-boxes, motion, etc., cylinder oil for the valves and pistons, and burning oil for the lamps, etc. superheater engines will also require special oil.

For local and shunting service the oil supply is usually calculated on the mileage and number of hours the engine is actually working, shunting engines in goods yards being reckoned at 6 or 8 miles per hour. Neath storekeeper also has charge of all the hand tools, taps, dies, reamers, etc., and must record the loan of any of these to the men on a slate or in a book, making sure of their return in good condition.

It is a good policy for the head storekeeper to confer with the foreman fitter and boilermaker every 14 days or so, and take stock of the stores account to see what items require replacement. Copper piping, white metal, metallic packing, brushes, springs, boiler tubes, brake blocks, fire-bricks and clay, etc., demand careful survey. In Neath shed a good system is in vogue whereby no issues of renewals are made from stores without a printed 'request' signed by the foreman and accompanied by the old article for inspection. Files in particular should be dealt with in this manner.

Petroleum oil has entirely superseded tallow for cleaning purposes; it is much cheaper and has not the detrimental action on the varnish and paint often resulting from the use of tallow.

In like manner sponge-cloths have taken the place of waste on many railways, and are systematically dealt with in a suitable laundry. They are tied together in bundles and dispatched in large waterproof bags to the laundry, whence they are returned in similar manner for reissue after washing. To replenish the stock and provide for wear and tear, one or two new cloths are allowed each driver and fireman daily, and they must return the dirty ones to stores before new ones are issued to them.

Mechanical Foreman
Fitting staff

The fitting staff are responsible for all running repairs being dealt with satisfactorily and to time. The foremen should endeavour to get everything done as expeditiously as possible to obviate friction among the staff and facilitate the departure of engines at their booked times.

The repairs undertaken in a running shed may be classified under four heads, as follows: (1) 'Heavy' repairs, varying according to the miles run, etc., (2) 'moderate' repairs, which will depend largely on the nature of the service on which the engine has been engaged; (3) 'light' or shed repairs requiring only casual treatment; (4) boiler repairs.

Heavy Repairs

These are influenced by the mileage made by the engine since its last overhaul, and when undertaken will certainly necessitate its being withdrawn from service for five or six weeks, depending on the class of engine and nature of work on which it has been engaged. The wheels of both engine and tender will need re-turning, axle-boxes will have to be refitted, steam-ports of cylinders faced up, valves and pistons examined, slide-bars adjusted, motion overhauled, etc. further, the eccentric sheaves should be removed from the crank-axle to enable the latter to be thoroughly examined; all the boiler mountings should also be inspected and tested.

Moderate Repairs

These may be taken as those occupying a week or so to carry out. They would include examination of injectors, valves and pistons, changing springs, rejointing steam-pipes, etc.

Chargehand Boilersmith

Light, or shed, repairs

These refer to those items booked by the driver, after he has made his regular examination of all the assembled parts of the engine, which he considers necessary to be done before it is taken out again. These entries receive the attention of the fitting and boiler-making foremen, who give instructions to their men regarding the best and most expeditious manner of executing the repairs. The details vary and may involve attention to almost any part of the locomotive, such as brake blocks requiring to be changed, springs defective, glands blowing, valves leaking, etc. After attention has been given to the details reported, the fitter or boilermaker entrusted with the work must sign 'off' the book to show the work has been done.

Chargehand Boilersmith
Boilersmith – Boiler Washers

Washing out

The effectual washing out of boilers is most important and considerably affects their efficiency. Each engine should have a 'wash-out' day every week, and care should be taken that the operation is properly performed. Carelessness will result in accumulation of dirt in the water-spaces, on the tubes and over the crown of the fire-box. These deposits will act as non-conductors of heat and prevent the boiler steaming well, although extra fuel may be consumed. Priming, too, is often caused by a dirty boiler, and delay may ensue from this and the attendant evil of lubricant being flooded out of the cylinders and valve chests. After a boiler has been washed out it should be inspected by the leading boilersmith, who should satisfy himself that all the loose dirt has been removed.

In Neath running sheds it is the practice to wash out and refill the boiler with hot water, in which case steam is raised and the engine returned to the road more rapidly. When this is done the hosepipes should be of a very substantial character, and flexible metallic hose is much used for the purpose. The water-tanks of the engines should also be periodically washed out, lads being sent in to clear away any matter which may have gathered round the feed connection orifices. Engines fitted with 'pick-up' arrangements often suffer from accumulations of fallen leaves.

Chargehand Boilersmith
Archmen   –   Tubers   –   Boiler-washers   –   Fire-lighters
Shed-labourers   –   Odd Grades

The term 'semi-skilled' is generally applied to those men deputed to repair engine and tender foot-boards, renew bricks, fire-arches, etc.

Fire-lighters or steam-raisers have to attend to the lighting up on fires in all engines required for service during the time they are on duty, and must also watch all the engines standing in steam as spare, etc., keeping up the water-level and doing other necessary work. Bar boys usually received their instructions from the fire-lighters as to engines of which they are to clean down the tube-plates, renew the fire-bars, and so on.

Another grade found in Neath running-sheds are the 'shed labourers', a useful class of workers assisting the fitters and boiler-makers on their various jobs, lifting engines, attending to hot boxes, etc. they are also employed in cleaning up the pits and shed, loading up ashes, drying sand in the furnace, and sifting it before use. From these men a number are often selected for attachment to the breakdown gang, accompanying the accident train to derailments and other mishaps

Tube sweepers are specially deputed to sweep tubes, an operation required to be performed more or less frequently, according to the coal burned. Clean tubes are necessary to secure a free-steaming engine and, further, neglect of the tubes will possibly result in the ends being burnt away.

Miscellaneous Work

The blacksmiths' work appertaining to a running-shed consists chiefly in repairing and adjusting brake work, straightening guard-irons, shortening or lengthening eccentric rods for the fitters, repairing fire-irons, prickers, darts, etc., attending to couplings and straightening buffer-beams, etc.

The copper-smiths will mainly be called upon to attend to steam and water pipes and connections, braze on flanges, and renew air and vacuum-brake pipes; they are also required to re-metal or line big-end brasses, axle-boxes, etc.

Notes on Shed Staff and Procedure

One fitter and one mate will maintain 6-8 engines in running order. The number of boilermakers required will, of course, depend on the quality of water used; on an average, one boilermaker can maintain 20-30 boilers, whilst one 'tuber' and assistant will be required for 15-20 boilers.

Typical Break-down Gang

One fitter, one tool attendant, two men for jacks, two men for packing, one steam-crane driver; total eight men.

The Blacksmith shop at Court Sart shed.   *Gerald*

Appendix Four

Swansea Docks

Swansea Docks Rail System
North Dock opened 1852
South Dock opened 1859
East Dock opened 1881 Prince of Wales (POW) Dock from 1884
King's Dock opened 1909
Queen's Dock opened 1920

Dock Shunting Contractors
Powesland & Mason 1881-1924 (Powesland & Mason main contractor to GWR)
South Dock Base – Shed Burrows Yard
W. Westlake (Riverside) 1886-1900 (Westlake Contractor to SHT and RSB)
Chris Rowland (POW) 1891-1905 (Rowland main contractor for Midland Railway and LNWR)
Swansea Harbour Trust (POW) 1905-1912
Swansea Harbour trust (POW) New Shed 1912-1930
Chris Rowland (Riverside) Second Shed 1905-1911
South Wales Railway (North Dock) 1852-1874
Vale of Neath Railway (Riverside High Level) 1863-1881 (Vale of Neath Railway Contractor to GWR for docks traffic until 1881)
Rhondda & Swansea Bay Railway (RSB) (Riverside) 1894-1889
GWR Swansea East Dock 1893-1964
RSB (New Shed) Danygraig 1896-1960 (RSB into dock 14th March, 1895)
Station opened 1896, station re-organized 1899

The first Swansea Harbour Trust (SHT) shed was the old Rowland shed when the Trust took over their dock works. They built their own new shed in 1912 in the Prince of Wales Dock, top end, and closed in 1930, the GWR took over the shed in 1923. The GWR took over all dock work by 1924.

Danygraig (87C)
Open 1896-closed 1960; remaining duties and locomotives transferred to Swansea East Dock.

Dock Duties
14T South Dock Low Level
14T Replenish Duty
King's Dock Rheola Patent Fuel Works
1 Pilot Day Shift
T4 – T6 – T8 – Low Level – 19T – 23T – tips, all dock duties
'11XX' locomotives working King's, Queen's etc.
Low Level work '57XX' on tips
20T on Tir John Tripper '57XX'
Jersey Pilot 3 turns '84XX'
Jersey Pilot used to bank trains on triangle; No. 4299 worked hump yard

Two Links
1 Shunting Link
1 Dock Link
1 Train turn: 3.30 pm Swansea Docks train of empties for Cymmer via RSB, banker from Aberavon. Coal return
In 1959 a diesel shunter was tried on dock
Class '08' diesel Jersey Yard 1963/64

On shed at Danygraig in May 1953 are GWR 0-6-0PT No. 4666 and ex-Swansea Harbour Trust 0-4-0ST No 1142. To the right and behind No. 1142 are two members of the GWR-built '1101' class 0-4-0T.   *T.J. Edgington*

In 1952 these locomotives were recorded at Danygraig:
Nos. 1101-1106 Dock locomotives
Nos. 1141-1145 Dock locomotives
Nos. 1634-1643 Small Panniers
Nos. 2146-2151 Burry Port locomotives
No. 4299 For Hump shunting
Ten Panniers '57XX' type 0-6-0 and No. 359 *Hilda* formerly Llanelly & Mynydd Mawr 0-6-0 locomotive
No. 1 *Hercules* (BR No. 2082) from Ystalyfera Tin Works

East Dock Loco

(1955) Locomotives present:
1104, 1140, 1152, 1652, 1641
Dock Targets – 5T Prince of Wales
26T South Dock High Level
27T Prince of Wales
17T South Dock Low Level
Locomotives worked out of Danygraig and Swansea East Dock; all work after January 1960 covered by Swansea East Dock.

Building History of Swansea Dock locomotives

Nos. 1101-1106 GWR
Nos. 1140-1147 Swansea Harbour Trust (SHT)
Nos. 1151-1153 Powesland & Mason (PM)

Nos. 1101-1106 Avonside 1926 for GWR (withdrawn 1959 (1101) remainder in 1960)
Nos. 1140-1141 Barclay for SHT 1905 (withdrawn 1958 and 1952 respectively)
No. 1142 Hudswell, Clarke for SHT 1911 (withdrawn 1959)
No. 1143 Peckett for SHT 1908 (withdrawn 1960)
No. 1144 Hawthorn, Leslie 1909 for SHT (withdrawn 1960)
No. 1145 Peckett for SHT 1918 (withdrawn 1959)
Nos. 1146-1147 Peckett for SHT 1912 (withdrawn 1951)
Nos. 1151-1152 Peckett for SHT 1907 (withdrawn 1963 and 1962 respectively)
Nos. 1153 Hawthorn, Leslie for SHT 1903 (withdrawn 1955)

Neath & Brecon List of Signal Boxes
(1945 until further notice)

Neath Riverside to Brecon (times during which boxes are open)

Distance Box to Box		Name of Box	Open* (Weekdays)	Closed (Weekdays)	Open (Sundays)	Closed (Sundays)
m.	ch.					
		Neath & Brecon Jn	5.00 am	Continuously until		5.00 am
					1.00 pm	1.30 pm
					8.30 pm	11.15 pm
	31	Neath Yard	3.30 am ⎫	After		–
	31 ½	Cadoxton	3.30 am ⎪	the		–
1	46 ¾	Cilfrew	3.45 am ⎪	last		–
2	15 ¾	Crynant	4.00 am ⎬	train		–
2	46 ½	Ynysdawley	4.15 am ⎪	Saturday		–
2	16	Onllwyn	4.30 am ⎭	night		–
	66	Colbren Jn	5.00 am	12.00 night		–
3	23 ¾	Craig-y-Nos	8.30 am	7.15 pm		–
10	4 ¼	Devynock	8.15 am	6.50 pm		–
8	54 ½	Brecon (Free St)	5.20 am	10.35 pm		–

Colbren Jn to Ynysygeinon Jn

		Colbren Jn	5.00 am	12.00 night		–
4	54	Ystradgynlais	7.00 am	10.00 pm		–

Neath Jn to Swansea Eastern Depot

		Neath Jn	3.40 am	Continuously until		5.30 am
	33 ¾	Neath & Brecon Jn	See above			
2	16 ¼	Cardonnel Jn		Open continuously		
	57	Jersey Marine Jn S.		Open continuously		
	71 ½	Briton Ferry Rd	6.00 am	Continuously until		6.00 am
1	14	Pritchard's Sdg		Open continuously		
	43	Burrow's Sdg		Open continuously		
	33	Prince of Wales Dock Jn	6.00 am	10.00 pm		–
	52 ½	Port Tennant Jn		Open continuously		
	25 ¼	Eastern Depot	6.00 am	Continuously until		6.00 am

* Monday mornings in the case of boxes which remain open through the week, or each weekday in the case of boxes not open for 24 hours each day.

Neath Riverside
(Winter 1951)

Arr.	Dep.	Class	Time	From	To	Remarks
00/53		J Freight	23.30	Glynneath	Eastern Depot	
02/43		J Freight	22.30	Aberdare	Eastern Depot	
04/08		J Freight	00.15	Aberdare	Eastern Depot	RR
04/32		J Freight	03.05	Eastern Depot	Glynneath	Return of 23.30 Glynneath
	05.50	B W/men	05.50		Glynneath	
	06.00	B W/men	06.00		Colbren Jn	
07.20		B W/men	06.35	Colbren Jn		Empty to Colbren for 08.10 (?)
07.33		B W/men	07.12	Glynneath		
	08.25	B Passenger	08.25		Brecon	
08/38		D Freight	05.20	Little Mill	Llanelli	via Cardonnel Jn
08.48		B Passenger	08.10	Colbren Jn		
08.55		B Auto	07.20	Ystrad Mynych		
	09.15	C Ety Auto	09.15		Neath General	
09/26		H Freight	07.15	Llandilo Jn	Hereford	
10.06		B Passenger	08.30	Brecon		
10/52		J Freight	08.10	Gadlys Jn	Carmarthen Jn	via Cardonnel Jn
11/36		J Freight	07.50	Carmarthen Jn	Aberdare	
15/13		K Freight	14.00	Eastern Depot	Glynneath	
15.43		B W/men	15.00	Colbren Jn		
15.56		C Pcls Auto	15.50	Neath General		
	16.10	B Passenger	16.10		Brecon	
	16.20	B Auto	16.20		Aberdare H L	
17.41		B Passenger	17.00	Colbren Jn		
18/11		K Empties	17.15	Eastern Depot	Aberdare	
19/53		C Ballast	18.20	Merthyr	Whitland	RR
19.54		B Pass./Mail	18.20	Brecon		
20/03		H Freight	15.10	Little Mill	Llandilo Jn	
20/08		K Freight		Glynneath	Eastern Depot	Return of 14.00 E Dp
	21.40	B Passenger	21.40		Colbren Jn	
23/51		K Freight	21.20	Eastern Depot	Neath Jn	No. 22 Control train

No. 25 Control Train works from Jersey South at 06.30 to Felin Fran then to Cardonnel Jn then to Neath Junction then back to Cardonnel and Jersey Marine.

Neath Gen Depart	Glynneath Depart	Neath Gen Arrive
22.00 (SX)	23.15 (SX)	23.41 (SX)
22.45 (SO)	23.20 (SO)	23.38 (SO)

Notes:
/ - passing time
RR Run as Required
SX Saturdays excepted
SO Saturdays only
W/men Workmen's train

Neath Passenger Turns on the Vale of Neath (1955)

Loco off shed for 7.40 am Neath to Pontypool Road

		am	
Neath	*dep.*	7.40	
Glyn Neath		8.00	
Aberdare		8.33-8.35	
Pontypool Road	*arr.*	9.43	(turn loco)
	dep.	11.00	
		pm	
Aberdare		12.10-12.12	
Glyn Neath		12.37	
Neath	*arr.*	12.55	Loco to shed
	dep.	1.00	Swansea men work to Swansea
Swansea	*arr.*	1.16	

		pm	
Swansea	*dep.*	3.00	Swansea set, off at Neath
Neath	*arr.*	3.21	Loco from shed
	dep.	3.37	
Glyn Neath		3.49	
Aberdare	*arr.*	4.26	Neath set off at Aberdare, walk to shed to prep engine for back working Gadlys Goods to Margam. Aberdare men work through to Pontypool Road and return
	dep.	4.35	
Pontypool Road	*arr.*	5.54	
	dep.	6.20	
Aberdare		7.30-7.35	
Glyn Neath		8.00	
Neath arr.		8.20	
Neath dept.		9.10	
Aberdare arr.		9.58	(M-F)

On Saturdays stock works through to Pontypool Road. Locomotive change at Aberdare (Pontypool Road men work forward on the 8.30 Pontypool Road to Aberdare arrive 9.47, return on the 10.05 to Pontypool Road, arrive 11.09).

Locomotive Allocations

Neath 87A 1960

Panniers		Large panniers	'42XX'/'52XX'	Other tank engines
1645	7786	8418	4242	4169
3611	7799	9430	4255	8104
3621	8715	9446	4264	6641
3687	8732	9448	4275	6650
3741	8760	9452	4279	
3757	8782	9473	4281	
3766	8784	9479	4282	
3774	9627		4283	
4653	9734		4284	
5720	9750		4288	
5761	9761		4295	
5773	9779		5222	
5779	9783		5239	
7739	9784		5242	
7757	9792			

14 panniers were outstabled at N&B shed (12) and Glyn Neath (2); total 55 locomotives.

Swansea East Dock 87D 1960

Panniers		Large panniers	'42XX'/'52XX'/'72XX'	Other tank engines
3641	6749	8414	4232	1151
3661	6753	8431	4271	1152
5704	6762	8475	5210	5616
6700	6763	8476	5211	5628
6702	6767	8483	5232	5675
6712	6768	9431	5246	6613
6714	7408	9433	5225	6662
6719	7704	9489	7226	
6720	9625		7248	
6738	9744			

Duffryn Yard 87K 1962/63

Panniers		Large panniers	'42XX'/'52XX' '72XX'		Other tank engines	Diesel shunters
3613	8724	8407	4213	5254	5670	D3432
3642	8746	8416	4250	7243	5688	D3433
3688	9617	8482	4256	7249	6620	D3434
3692	9634	8490	4286		6680	D3435
3718	9671	9454	4296		6686	D3436
3762	9715	9456	4299		6691	D3437
3791	9734	9457	5216			D3438
4684	9742	9464	5228			
4695	9766	9483	5230			
5728	9785		5232			
5787	9799		5246			

BR Standard pacific No. 70023 *Venus* approaches Neath with the up 'Pembroke Coast Express'
in 1958.   *Norman Jones*

A 'Castle' class in the full flight with the up 'Pembroke Coast Express' as it approaches Neath,
first stop Cardiff. This view was taken from the signal box.   *Norman Jones*

Appendix Nine

Some Crack Expresses

The 'Capitals United Express'

The 'Capitals United Express' was introduced on 6th February, 1956. The name was withdrawn on September 1965.

1957 timings

		am				pm	
Swansea	*dep.*	6.30		Paddington	*dep.*	3.55	
Neath	*arr.*	6.45		Newport	*arr.*	6.33	
	dep.	6.48			*dep.*	6.36	
Port Talbot	*arr.*	6.58		Cardiff	*arr.*	6.53	*Loco change*
	dep.	7.00			*dep.*	7.00	
Bridgend	*arr.*	7.18		Bridgend	*arr.*	7.31	
	dep.	7.21			*dep.*	7.33	
Cardiff	*arr.*	7.50		Port Talbot	*arr.*	7.51	
	dep.	8.00			*dep.*	7.53	
Newport	*arr.*	8.18		Bridgend	*arr.*	8.06	
	dep.	8.20			*dep.*	8.08	
Paddington	*arr.*	10.50		Swansea	*arr.*	8.26	

Typical stock used on this and the other non-Pullman South Wales expresses until 1965 would have been Hawksworth 1944 stock with a tare weight of 32 tons. Also used were ex-GWR 'Sunshine Stock' 32 ton coaches. The 'Sunshine Stock' vehicles were built between 1936 and 1940 and were withdrawn in 1965. The older (1935-built) and heavier (33 ton) Centenary stock also saw service until its withdrawal from 1964 onwards. The heaviest vehicles of all were the restaurant cars which weighed 40 tons and were carried on six-wheel bogies. The passenger brake vans had a tare weight of 30 tons. By 1967 all ex-GWR coaching stock had been withdrawn from main line working with restaurant cars being the last to be replaced.

The 'Pembroke Coast Express'

The 'Pembroke Coast Express' was introduced on 5th June, 1953. Promoted as Wales' fastest train, at one time this service was timed London to Swansea in 3 hours 45 minutes and Swansea to London in four hours. The run non-stop from London to Newport (133.4 miles) was timed at 131 minutes, an average speed of 62.5 mph. The locomotive used on the up service would return on the down 'South Wales Pullman' the following morning. The 'Pembroke Coast Express' was taken out of service on 7th September, 1963.

1957 timings

		pm				am	
Pembroke Dock	*dep.*	1.05		Paddington	*dep.*	10.55	
Swansea	*arr.*	3.38	*Loco change*	Newport	*arr.*	1.43	*pm*
	dep.	3.45			*dep.*	1.46	
Cardiff	*arr.*	4.53		Cardiff	*arr.*	2.04	
	dep.	5.00			*dep.*	2.10	
Newport	*arr.*	5.17		Swansea	*arr.*	3.18	
	dep.	5.20					
Paddington	*arr.*	7.45					

An unidentified 'Castle' class 4-6-0 runs through Neath with the up 'Red Dragon'. The Vale of Neath line veers off to the right. *Norman Jones*

An unidentified 'Hall' class 4-6-0 powers the 'Red Dragon' non-stop through Neath passing the unusual Neath signal box which was clad with flat panels and built in 1929 to replace an earlier Neath Station signal box (*see page 14*). *Norman Jones*

The 'Red Dragon'

The 'Red Dragon' was introduced on 5th June, 1950. It was the heaviest of the named expresses and usually consisted of 12 bogies (approx. 400 tons) - more on Summer Saturdays. The name was withdrawn in September 1965.

1957 timings

		am				*pm*	
Swansea	*dep.*	8.45		Paddington	*dep.*	5.55	
Cardiff	*arr.*	9.42	*Loco change*	Newport	*arr.*	8.47	
	dep.	10.00			*dep.*	8.50	
Newport	*arr.*	10.18		Cardiff	*arr.*	9.07	*Loco change*
	dep.	10.21			*dep.*	9.18	
Paddington	*arr.*	1.00 *pm*		Bridgend	*arr.*	9.46	
					dep.	9.48	
				Port Talbot	*arr.*	10.06	
					dep.	10.08	
				Bridgend	*arr.*	10.19	
					dep.	10.22	
				Swansea	*arr.*	10.38	

The 'South Wales Pullman' and 'Blue Pullmans'

The 'South Wales Pullman' was introduced on 27th June, 1955. The train was limited to eight super saloons (328 tons). On Friday 8th September, 1961 Neath-allocated 'Castle' class 4-6-0 No. 4080 *Dorchester Castle* worked the last steam-hauled 'South Wales Pullman'. 'Blue Pullmans' took over the service on Monday 11th September until May 1973.

1957 timings

		pm			*am*
Swansea	*dep.*	4.31	Paddington	*dep.*	8.50
Neath	*arr.*	4.47	Newport	*dep.*	11.22
	dep.	4.49	Cardiff	*arr.*	11.40
Port Talbot	*arr.*	4.59		*dep.*	11.45
	dep.	5.01	Bridgend	*arr.*	12.16 *pm*
Bridgend	*arr.*	5.18		*dep.*	12.18
	dep.	5.20	Port Talbot	*arr.*	12.36
Cardiff	*arr.*	5.52		*dep.*	12.39
	dep.	6.00	Bridgend	*arr.*	12.49
Newport	*arr.*	6.18		*dep.*	12.51
	dep.	6.21	Swansea	*arr.*	1.10
Paddington	*arr.*	8.45			

On the introduction of 'Blue Pullmans' the timings were revised. New timings were:

06.40   Swansea to Paddington
16.55   Paddington to Swansea.

From   June 1967 a second Pullman set ran, its timimgs were:

09.00   Paddington to Swansea
16.20   Swansea to Paddington.

There was also a 'Cardiff Pullman' from June 1964 until 3rd November, 1969:

11.00   Paddington to Cardiff
14.30   Cardiff to Paddington

A 'Castle' class 4-6-0 with the Hawksworth tender passes through Briton Ferry at speed with the up 'South Wales Pullman'.   *Norman Jones*

The 4.31 pm from Swansea 'Blue Pullman' waits for the 'right away' from the temporary platform at Port Talbot in 1963.   *C. Read*

Appendix Ten

Goods Trains from Swansea East Dock (1957)

2.30 am to Cardiff
Engine/Van to Jersey, depart at 3.47, work to Margam Upside (pick up traffic), Bridgend Upside (pick up traffic), Penarth Curve, leave train in yard engine to shed, train crew travel home passenger (THP).

3.15 am to Cardiff (Ely Sidings)
Load traffic from Swansea Docks or Jersey, pick up bogie bolster traffic for Tyseley, work to Ely Sdgs pick up traffic, train crew relief at Canton.
Train crew THP.

6.05 am to Cardiff
Load London coal (Acton Yards) from Jersey, relief at Canton, report to control for back working.

6.30 am to Tondu
Work empty coal wagons (pools) from Swansea Docks to Tondu, work coal back to docks.

6.55 am to Saltney (Vac. Train)
Load empty vans from Swansea Docks or Jersey Marine Jn via Neath Jn, relief at Pontypool Road (THP).

7.15 am Control Train
Work traffic between Margam and Swansea Docks as ordered.

8.45 am to Aberdare
Book on and walk to Swansea High St, travel passenger on the 9.45 am High St to Pontypool Road as far as Aberdare, driver and fireman pick up locomotive at Aberdare shed, guard walk to Gadlys Sidings to take tally of train, engine from shed to Gadlys Sidings, work coal traffic to Swansea Docks for shipment.

9.30 am to Morlais Colliery (Control Train)
Work coal empties from Swansea Docks to the colliery and return with shipment coal.

10.00 am to Severn Tunnel Jn
Work London coal traffic (Acton Yards) from Jersey Marine Jn to Canton, relief by Cardiff men, return home passenger on the 2.10 pm Cardiff to Swansea stopping train.

10.15 am Control Train
Work traffic to and from Cwmfelin Works, Landore, as ordered.

11.00 am Control Train
Work traffic to and from Pembrey Power Station, as ordered.

12.15 pm Skewen Control Train
Work traffic from Swansea docks (Burrows Sdgs) to South Dock-High St Goods-Six Pit - Skewen, shunt yards return Six Pit-Landore Down Side-South Dock-Port Tennant. Engine to shed.

1.00 pm (Tin Train) London Vac. Train
Traffic from Burrows Yard (sheet metal in vans)-Wind St Jn (run round train)-High St Goods-Neath Yard-Margam Upside, train crew relief at Canton (THP).

2.10 pm Control Train
Report to control for work.

5.00 pm Graig Control Train
Work traffic from Swansea Docks to Graig Merthy Colliery and return with coal traffic.

5.15 pm to Aberdare
Work coal empties (pools) from Swansea Dock to Aberdare and return with shipment coal.

5.50 pm Margam Control Train
Works traffic between Swansea Docks and Margam, as ordered.

8.00 pm Control Train
Report to control for work.

9.25 pm to Neyland (Vac. Train)
Work traffic from Port Tennant, pick up at Jersey Marine Jn, pick up at Felin Fran, pick up at Llanelli Yard (next to station). Depot men came off at Llanelli (THP).

'42XX' class 2-6-2T No. 5222 of Neath shed hauls a rake of empty mineral wagons from Swansea Docks towards Briton Ferry on 12th May, 1960. The bridge is the old South Wales Mineral Railway bridge into Court Sart yard. *John Hodge*

Appendix Eleven

Shed Closures

1959	(31st August) Paxton Street (although it remained in use for two years to service engines off the Central Wales line).
1961	(June) Landore closed to steam
1962	(31st December) Brecon
1963	(4th February) Upper Bank
1964	(March) Neath N&B closed to steam. Diesel allocation Nos: 6881, 6913, 6930 also one '08' shunting diesel No.3745, two '69XX' diesels transferred from Glyn Neath 5th October, 1964
1964	(15th June) Neath Jn to Neath Bridge closed
1964	(5th October) Glyn Neath closed, men transferred to Neath N&B (with two diesels).
1965	(14th June) Neath 87A (diesels transferred to Neath station stabling point). 87A lost all its main line locomotives on 2nd November, 1964, leaving just shunting locomotives Nos: 3647, 3654, 3687, 4612, 4669, 9616, 9617, 9625, 9678, 6614 and 6628.
1969	(12th April) Neath N&B
1983	(May) Swansea East Dock (guards finished in July)

In 1965 one duty at N&B was still worked by steam with a Neath pannier 9.10 N&B Yard (New sidings) to Resolven and Glyn Neath, returning to depot at 6.05 pm.

The last remaining steam locomotives at N&B shed were Nos. 4297 and 5261 working the N&B coal traffic, they went to Cardiff East Dock in 1964.

'Hall' class 4-6-0 No. 6918 *Sandon Hall* at Landore shed on 9th September, 1951. Also on shed are an unidentified 'Star' class 4-6-0 and 'Modified Hall' No. 6959 *Peatling Hall*.

H.C. Casserley

Pannier tank No. 9642 at Maesteg colliery shed in 1969.   *Author's Collection*

Pannier tank No. 9642 in pieces at Baglan Bay works in 1987.   *Author*

Appendix Twelve

Pannier Tank No. 9642 Steams On

No. 9642 was built in Swindon works and was released into traffic in April 1946. It was initially allocated to Westbury and Frome sheds but was then transferred to Bridport and Weymouth. In 1956 it was sent to Abercynon and two years later it had moved on to St Philips Marsh, Bristol. The engine's final BR shed transfer was to Southall in 1959, where it remained until being taken out of traffic in 1964.

On withdrawal it was sent to Hayes scapyard at Tremains, Bridgend, where it was used as a yard shunter until the Jones brothers purchased the engine in 1968. No. 9642 was taken to Maesteg washery still in steaming capacity where it was used for brake van rides within the colliery system.

When the boiler ticket ran out it was put into the colliery engine shed for storage and then put up for sale. The South Wales Pannier Group purchased the locomotive in 1983 and it languished at Maesteg until removal to BP's Baglan Bay works where work progressed slowly out in the open supervised by engineer Mike Brannan. Covered accommodation was needed to progress the repairs and No. 9642 was then moved to the Swansea Vale engine shed at Upper Bank in 1989.

In 1996 the locomotive was ready for test running and, after a few minor adjustments, it was put into service on the local Swansea Vale Railway passenger trains where a few minor faults were attended to. No. 9642 was then put up for hire on the open market.

It eventually went to the Dean Forest Railway in 1998 which seemed to fulfil all the necessary requirements to maintain the engine and also had a running shed. After a few more adjustments to the engine it went into operational traffic in the summer of 1998 on Dean Forest passenger trains.

In steam once more. 0-6-0PT No. 9642 at Lydney station on the Dean Forest Railway in 1990.   *Author*

Posing in front of '78XX' class 4-6-0 No. 7802 *Bradley Manor* at the Severn Valley Railway in 2005 are, *from left to right*, Danny Counsell, John Pemberton, John Last and Gerald Williams. John Pemberton retired as train crew manager at Cardiff Canton.   *Author*

Bryan King, photographed in 2000 on the footplate of No. 1, a 1914-built Peckett 0-4-0ST of 1914 (Works No. 1345), on the Swansea Vale Railway.   *Alex Goulay*